Communications in Computer and Information Science   1338

More information about this series at http://www.springer.com/series/7899

Lejla Batina · Gang Li (Eds.)

Applications and Techniques in Information Security

11th International Conference, ATIS 2020
Brisbane, QLD, Australia, November 12–13, 2020
Proceedings

Editors
Lejla Batina ⓘ
Radboud University
Nijmegen, The Netherlands

Gang Li ⓘ
Deakin University
Geelong, VIC, Australia

ISSN 1865-0929   ISSN 1865-0937 (electronic)
Communications in Computer and Information Science
ISBN 978-981-33-4705-2   ISBN 978-981-33-4706-9 (eBook)
https://doi.org/10.1007/978-981-33-4706-9

This Springer imprint is published by the registered company Springer Nature Singapore Pte Ltd.
The registered company address is: 152 Beach Road, #21-01/04 Gateway East, Singapore 189721, Singapore

Preface

The International Conference on Applications and Techniques in Information Security (ATIS) has been held annually since 2010. This year was the 10th edition of the ATIS conference, which was set to be held in Brisbane, Queensland, Australia, but due to the travel restrictions imposed, ATIS 2020 was a fully virtual conference and held during November 12–13, 2020. ATIS 2020 focused on all aspects on techniques and applications in information security research, and provided a valuable connection between the theoretical and the implementation communities, thus attracting participants from industry and academia.

The selection process this year was competitive, we received 24 submissions, which reflects the recognition of, and interest in, this conference. Each submitted paper was reviewed by three members of the Program Committee. Following this independent review, there were discussions among reviewers and chairs. A total of 8 papers were selected as full papers, with an acceptance rate of 30%. Moreover, we were honored to have a prestigious scholar giving a keynote speech at the conference: Dr. Yuval Yarom, Senior Lecturer, School of Computer Science at The University of Adelaide, and Researcher in the Trustworthy Systems group at Data61, CSIRO, Australia, with keynote entitled "Whack-a-Meltdown: a Micro-Architectural Game."

We would like to thank everyone who participated in the development of the ATIS 2020 program. In particular, we give special thanks to the Program Committee and its chair, Professor Lejla Batina, Radboud University, The Netherlands, for their diligence and concern for the quality of the program, and also with their detailed feedback to the authors. The conference also relied on the efforts of the ATIS 2020 Organizing Committee. Especially, we thank Dr. Leonie Simpson, A/Professor Gang Li, Professor Lynn Batten, and Dr. Jiaojiao Jiang for the general administrative issues, the registration process, and the maintenance of the conference website.

Finally, and most importantly, we thank all the authors who submitted papers as they are the primary reason why ATIS 2020 is so exciting, and why it will be the premier forum in future for presentation and discussion of innovative ideas, research results, applications, and experience from around the world, as well as highlighting activities in related research areas. Because of your diligent work, ATIS 2020 was a great success.

October 2020

Lejla Batina
Lynn Batten

Organization

ATIS 2020 was organized by Science and Engineering Faculty | Queensland University of Technology, Brisbane, Queensland, Australia

Steering Committee

Lynn Batten (Chair)	Deakin University, Australia
Heejo Lee	Korea University, South Korea
Gang Li (Secretary)	Deakin University, Australia
Jiqiang Liu	Beijing Jiaotong University, China
Tsutomu Matsumoto	Yokohama National University, Japan
Wenjia Niu	Beijing Jiaotong University, China
Yuliang Zheng	University of Alabama at Birmingham, USA

Organizing Committee

General Co-chairs

Leonie Simpson	Queensland University of Technology, Australia
Lynn Batten	Deakin University, Australia

Program Committee Chair

Lejla Batina	Radboud University, The Netherlands

Awards Co-chairs

Lejla Batina	Radboud University, The Netherlands
Jiaojiao Jiang	UNSW Sydney, Australia

Publication Chairs

Lejla Batina	Radboud University, The Netherlands
Gang Li	Deakin University, Australia

Web Master

Jiaojiao Jiang	UNSW Sydney, Australia

Program Committee

Edilson Arenas	Central Queensland University, Australia
Leijla Batina	Radboud University, The Netherlands
Lynn Batten	Deakin University, Australia
Bernard Colbert	Deakin University, Australia

Rafiqul Islam	Charles Sturt University, Australia
Kwangjo Kim	KAIST, South Korea
Andrei Kelarev	Victoria University, Australia
Lei Pan	Deakin University, Australia
Jinqiao Shi	Chinese Academy of Sciences, China
Lisa Soon	Central Queensland University, Australia
Veelasha Moonsamy	Radboud University, The Netherlands
Brijesh Verma	Central Queensland University, Australia
Marilyn Wells	Central Queensland University, Australia
Tianqing Zhu	University of Technology Sydney, Australia
Xun Yi	RMIT University, Australia

Sponsoring Institutions

Deakin University, Australia
Queensland University of Technology, Australia
Radboud University, The Netherlands
ITSecurity Research, Victoria, Australia
CCIS, Springer, Cham, Switzerland

Contents

A Framework for Evaluation of Software Obfuscation Tools for Embedded Devices

Anjali J. Suresh[✉] and Sriram Sankaran

Center for Cybersecurity Systems and Networks, Amrita School of Engineering,
Amritapuri, India
{anjalijsuresh,srirams}@am.amrita.edu

Abstract. Obfuscation is a popular software transformation to protect intellectual property and avoid reverse engineering. It relies on introducing additional instructions and changing control-flow without affecting program semantics. This introduces overheads in terms of memory, execution time and energy consumption for resource-constrained embedded devices. In this work, we show that these overheads are dependent on three factors: the transformations and their combinations selected, the tool used to effect these transformations and the program workload. In addition, there exists a need for measuring the security of obfuscated code. In this work, we develop a framework for evaluating software obfuscation tools potentially highlighting costs and benefits associated with obfuscation and analyze energy-performance-security trade offs for embedded devices. Our experiments using two popular obfuscation tools, Obfuscation Low-Level Virtual Machine (OLLVM) and Tigress, show that obfuscation could potentially lead to a 5-fold increase in execution time and energy consumption depending on these factors. In addition, Tigress provides more security and simultaneously incurs significant energy consumption compared to OLLVM. Our cost-benefit analysis with respect to energy, performance and security can be used to determine the optimal choice of security measures for resource-constrained environments.

Keywords: Code obfuscation · Obfuscator Low Level Virtual Machine · Tigress · Intermediate representation · Energy consumption · Security · Potency · Resilience

1 Introduction

Obfuscation is a popular software transformation to protect intellectual property and avoid reverse engineering. It converts the source code to different form which is functionally equivalent and produces same output as that of the original source code. It relies on introducing additional instructions and changing control-flow without affecting program semantics thus increasing the complexity of the source code and making it pseudo-random.

© Springer Nature Singapore Pte Ltd. 2020
L. Batina and G. Li (Eds.): ATIS 2020, CCIS 1338, pp. 1–13, 2020.
https://doi.org/10.1007/978-981-33-4706-9_1

While obfuscation provides time-limited protection for embedded devices, it is necessary to analyze the energy consumption of obfuscated code. Obfuscation introduces additional instructions or control flow paths through the program thus making it difficult to reverse engineer the source code. This leads to overheads in terms of energy consumption, execution time and storage of the program. Since obfuscation introduces overheads, using advanced forms of obfuscation for applications that run on embedded devices which are typically resource-constrained may be infeasible. Even for simpler forms of obfuscation, it may be necessary to limit the extent to which it is applied to transform the application.

In addition, there exists a need for measuring the security of obfuscated code for resilience against numerous attacks. However, measuring the security is challenging due to the increasing complexity of obfuscated code. Complexity of obfuscated code is generally described by potency and resilience. Potency measures the complexity imposed by obfuscation and resilience denotes the difficulty of the attacker to de-obfuscate the source code. These collectively emphasize the need for a framework to measure energy, performance and security of obfuscated code and analyze the trade-offs for embedded devices.

In this paper, we study the impact of obfuscation techniques, tools and program workload on the overheads introduced by obfuscation. We study the impact of obfuscation techniques such as Control Flow Flattening, Bogus Control Flow and Instruction Substitution, on energy, performance and security overheads. To control variance in overheads due to the tool, we study two tools that implement these transformations: the OLLVM obfuscator tool [1], which is based on LLVM compiler infrastructure [2], and the commercially available Tigress obfuscator [3]. As obfuscation tends to increase the number of instructions and the cyclomatic complexity while producing a semantically equivalent program, we also consider the impact of the program workload of different sizes and varying parameters on energy-performance-security and analyzing energy-performance-security trade-offs of obfuscated programs.

2   Related Work

There are numerous research works done in code obfuscation and different approaches to measure the energy consumption for obfuscated code. Behera and Bhaskari [4] discusses some of the obfuscation methods, which can help to protect the sensitive code fragments of any software, without alteration of inherent functionalities of the software. Balakrishnan and Schulze [5] surveyed the different obfuscation techniques that are currently being researched and review the types of viruses that commonly use obfuscation and the techniques they employ. Dong *et al.* [6] provides a board view of Android obfuscation techniques and designed detection models for each obfuscation technique.

Different obfuscation tools are existing for both hardware based and software based obfuscation. Obfuscation Low Level Virtual Machine (OLLVM) [7] is a prototype tool which is based on LLVM Intermediate Representation (IR). Tigress [3] is a code-to-code obfuscator which implements different kinds of protection against both static and dynamic analysis. ProGuard [8] only focuses on remaining obfuscation which does not increase the security of the code. There exist numerous other obfuscators such as Allatori [9], Dasho [10], Zelix [11] are java obfuscators. [12] analyzed the Return-Oriented Programming (ROP) based attacks on code obfuscated by both OLLVM and tigress and compared their efficiency. In the paper [13], a comparison of the effectiveness of obfuscation is done by analyzing the dynamic behavior of code to find similarities between obfuscated and non-obfuscated code. This work also uses the same obfuscation tools, Obfuscator-LLVM and Tigress.

There are numerous mechanisms to measure the energy consumption of code. Khan *et al.* [14] and Sankaran [15] modeled the energy consumption of multi-core systems using a statistical learning approach. [16] modeled the energy consumption of embedded devices using performance counters. Grech *et al.* developed techniques for performing a static analysis on the intermediate compiler representations of a program [17]. It is important to focus on intermediate representation to bridge the gap between high level and low-level program structure. Đuković and Varga [18] measured energy consumption based on the load profiles and it is based on instruction level. Sankaran and Gupta [19] developed an approach to analyze power-performance trade-offs for mobile devices. Sahin *et al.* [20] conducted an analysis on energy consumption of different obfuscations on Android applications on four different mobile phone platforms. They proved the significant impact of obfuscation on energy consumption. Raj, Jithish, and Sankaran [21] impact of code obfuscation is measured with respect to energy consumption. They have used transformations such as lexical, data and control flow transformations and used one obfuscation tool.

Evaluating the effectiveness and resilience of the obfuscated code are important in the case of code obfuscation. Viticchié *et al.* [22] evaluated the resilience of the obfuscated code by performing two attacks and analyzed the time taken to attack the obfuscated and non-obfuscated code. They evaluated the efficiency of the VarMerge obfuscation which is one of the data obfuscation techniques. Banescu, Collberg, and Pretschner [23] developed a framework for choosing relevant features for estimating the effect of automated attacks and predict the resilience of the obfuscated code against automated attacks. They choose a subset of features based on computing personal correlations and variable importance in regression models. Wu *et al.* [24] built an evaluation model based on a regression model to evaluate the security of the obfuscated code. It also selects the security strength for each obfuscation method based on the security score obtained from this model. They measured potency for metrics such as software complexity metrics, transform model, multi-thread factor and diversity.

Existing research works are concentrated on energy-performance of a single obfuscation tool and evaluated the transformations. In this work, we compare the efficiency and performance of two most popular obfuscation tools such as OLLVM and Tigress. We choose these two tools because OLLVM is platform and language independent while Tigress is platform dependent and processes C code. We use C source code applications for testing purposes as C language is supported by both obfuscation tools. We analyse whether the dependency on the platform can affect energy consumption and performance.

3   Experimental Set-Up

In this section, we describe tools used for power measurement, benchmark applications and metrics used for analyzing energy-performance-security trade-offs.

3.1   Power Measurement

We use Powerstat [25] for power measurements. It is a linux tool which computes power consumption of Laptop when running on battery. It shows the current power consumption rate in energy units per second. Its output depends on the system's load and shows power consumption statistics. It shows information such as time, user, nice, sys (CPU usage), idle, IO protocol, running processes, context switch rate, IRQ/s, fork, exec, exit and watts. It is available in Ubuntu Linux.

3.2   Benchmarks

We consider the applications in Table 1 from the Mibench [26] benchmark suite for analyzing the impact of code obfuscation on energy usage, execution time and storage. For each of the benchmarks, we use three different sizes of the workload: small (S), medium (M) and large (L) as shown in Table 1. Small and medium sized data sets are available in the Mibench benchmarks and large sized data sets are available as open source.

Table 1. Benchmark applications

Application	Description	S	M	L
Qsort	Sorting an array of numbers	53	1536	2,36,700
Basicmath	Mathematical calculations such as cubic function, square root evaluation, degrees to radian conversion etc.	3	56	727
Susan	Image recognition package used to determine the position of edges and corners	8	109	16,000
String search	Searching a string in an array of already defined strings	3	56	727
Dijkstra	Find shortest paths from source to all vertices	4	49	73,000
Patricia	Find longest-prefix matching	247	1,479	50,200
SHA	Transforming data into a 160-bit message digest	305	3,172	10,234

3.3   Tools

For our experiments we use OLLVM and Tigress as our obfuscation tools. The OLLVM obfuscator uses the LLVM intermediate representation, and consequently, supports all programming languages which can be transformed to the

LLVM intermediate representation. Tigress [3] is a free code-to-code obfuscator for C programming language. It supports defenses against reverse engineering and attacks. Tigress offers features such as control ow attending with different dispatching techniques, function splitting and merging, virtualization with a randomly-generated instruction set and data encoding. In this work, we comparatively analyze energy-performance-security trade-offs of obfuscated code for two obfuscation tools, OLLVM and Tigress.

3.4 Metrics

Energy: We measure the average power and execution time and computed energy consumption using the following equation.

$$E_{prog} = P_{prog} \times T_{prog} \tag{1}$$

where E_{prog}, P_{prog} and T_{prog} stands for energy consumption, power consumption and execution time of the program respectively.

Performance: We measure performance based on execution time and storage for varying input sizes. In particular, execution time was computed by adding clock() function in the beginning and end of the code.

$$P_{exec} = \frac{P_{end} - P_{start}}{t1} \tag{2}$$

where P_{exec} is the program execution time, P_{end} is the program ended time, P_{start} is the program beginning time and t1 is CLOCKS_PER_SEC (the number of clock ticks per second).

Security: Security of obfuscated code is measured using two parameters such as potency and resilience. Potency is the amount of difficulty added to the code to understand. Resilience measures the difficulty of automatically breaking the obfuscated code.

Potency is measured in terms of general complexity and transform model. General complexity is measured by considering the complexities such as data flow, control flow, instruction and data complexity. Data flow complexity is calculated by the number of inter-basic block references. Control flow complexity is measured with respect to number of edges, branches and nodes in the control flow graph.

We adapt the strategy used to measure potency from [24] and resilience metric from [22]. We comparatively analyse energy-performance-security trade-offs of the code obfuscated by two obfuscation tools. Thus we conceal the research gap between the derived equations and energy-performance-security trade-offs. N-scope complexity is measured by

$$ns(\psi) = \frac{\sum_{B_i \in B} |R(\psi), B_i|}{\sum_{B_i \in B} |R(\psi), B_i| + |NC_\psi|} \tag{3}$$

where B is the set of branch blocks and NC_ψ is the node count in ψ and $R(\psi, B_i)$ is the nesting level the branch contributes.

Increase in control flow complexity is measured by

$$C_1 = \frac{ns(\psi')}{ns(\psi)} - 1 \tag{4}$$

where $ns(\psi')$ is N-scope complexity of obfuscated code and $ns(\psi)$ is N-scope complexity of non-obfuscated code.

Transform model describes that as the transform round increases security also increases because each round has impact on the input for next round. We use the transform model described in [24]

$$X = \frac{\sum\limits_{B_i \in B} |T(B_i')|}{\sum\limits_{B_i \in B} |T(B_i)|} - 1 \tag{5}$$

where T(B) is the number of transform rounds on block B.

Resilience measures the amount of effort taken for the attacker to deobfuscate the obfuscated code. Resilience of the obfuscated code is measured in terms of correctness, execution time and efficiency for deobfuscated code. We use Jakstab deobfuscation tool which is a static analysis for binary that produces the context free grammar of the original source code from the obfuscated code. The metrics which we considered for measuring the resilience are correctness, execution time and efficiency.

Correctness of deobfuscation is described as

$$Corr(T) = \begin{cases} 1 \text{ if task succeeded} \\ 0 \text{ task failed in task within given time} \end{cases} \tag{6}$$

Variable time: It is measured as the number of minutes spent by attacker to perform task T, successfully or not.

Efficiency variable: It is the sum of the inverse of the time taken to successfully performed the task T.

4   Energy Analysis

In this section, we analyze energy and performance of different obfuscation transformations of code obfuscated by OLLVM and tigress using Mibench benchmarks.

Table 2. Comparison of percentage overheads of obfuscating with OLLVM and Tigress tool. Here, F, B, I, and ALL stand for Control Flow Flattening, Bogus Control Flow, Instruction Substitution, all obfuscations applied together. S is storage overhead, and E_* and T_* stand for energy and run-time overhead respectively where $* \in \{\text{small}(s), \text{medium}(m), \text{large}(l)\}$ inputs. Details of input sizes provided in Table 1

App		S	E_s	T_s	E_m	T_m	E_l	T_l		S	E_s	T_s	E_m	T_m	E_l	T_l
Qsort	F	5	2	4	15	6	7	28	F+B	5	8	13	19	9	1	23
	B	5	9	2	9	4	16	40	F+I	5	3	6	19	6	4	71
	I	5	9	1	3	2	15	37	B+I	5	1	2	13	4	15	7
									ALL	5	16	20	25	7	3	12
Basicmath	F	7	27	5	25	15	7	28	F+B	18	9	29	40	19	14	26
	B	6	2	0.4	25	15	16	40	F+I	16	2	11	24	13	24	16
	I	4	3	2	26	12	15	37	B+I	20	4	11	3	9	20	12
									ALL	23	17	30	41	23	6	27
Susan	F	20	27	55	17	12	21	14	F+B	22	24	50	27	11	19	20
	B	20	46	57	48	43	22	22	F+I	27	10	77	36	24	74	15
	I	10	5	18	75	69	34	75	B+I	22	49	64	29	74	49	83
									ALL	34	19	47	44	49	3	8
String search	F	20	72	13	65	53	21	14	F+B	86	86	62	66	55	19	20
	B	20	7	19	97	74	22	22	F+I	47	85	54	39	27	74	15
	I	20	4	3	26	18	34	75	B+I	73	84	61	73	61	49	83
									ALL	90	91	72	93	87	3	8
Dijkstra	F	119	19	10	17	12	36	8	F+B	111	47	80	72	57	4	2
	B	111	35	10	79	94	29	55	F+I	127	29	70	61	46	11	15
	I	115	2	1	85	91	28	60	B+I	111	45	73	92	86	38	89
									ALL	125	12	73	96	47	10	12
Patricia	F	2	37	12	43	14	6	36	F+B	28	73	40	59	18	17	16
	B	5	15	10	47	22	88	84	F+I	37	41	75	50	16	18	15
	I	5	2	5	46	25	94	68	B+I	30	10	17	66	32	54	55
									ALL	30	70	44	71	29	8	7
SHA	F	16	141	6	21	18	0.3	1	F+B	34	70	54	23	15	17	16
	B	18	28	6	55	50	5	6	F+I	36	74	45	93	12	17	15
	I	11	85	6	99	92	2	11	B+I	31	9	62	73	61	54	55
									ALL	46	85	71	74	63	8	7

Impact of Obfuscation Scheme. The obfuscation scheme that we apply to the programs in our benchmark are listed in Table 2. They are the power set of the selected transformations—*Control Flow Flattening* (denoted as F), *Instruction Substitution* (denoted as I) and *Bogus Control Flow* (denoted as B). When we apply a scheme, we measure increase in size of source code due to the obfuscation as well as energy and performance overheads denoted by the E_* and T_* numbers where the subscripts denote the size of the workloads—small (s), medium (m) and large (l).

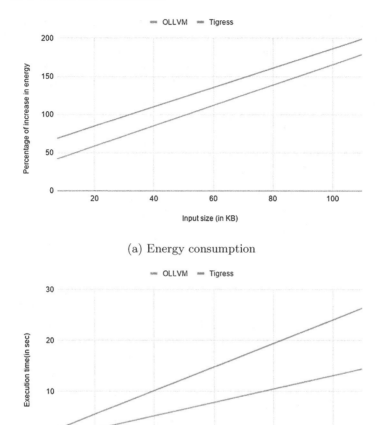

(a) Energy consumption

(b) Execution time

Fig. 1. Analysing the impact of energy consumption and execution time while input size is varied from 8kb to 109 kb for susan application

Our results show that obfuscation leads to higher energy consumption and increase in execution time. Using combinations of transformations leads to large numbers for non-functional properties when compared to single transformations. The largest numbers are generally when all the transformations are applied together. However, there are a couple of interesting points in the table. Firstly, it can be seen that, in some cases, Instruction Substitution can be applied with very little overhead. This is evident through comparable numbers for F+B and ALL for BasicMath, Susan, Patricia and SHA. Control Flow Flattening has the largest value for energy consumption and execution time. This is because it increases the number of loop operations which are computationally intensive costing additional energy and time. Bogus Control Flow leads to maximum increase in code size because new control flow paths are introduced in the program.

The second insightful trend is the dependence of these numbers on the size of the workload. Energy and performance figures deteriorate as the size of the workload increases for every obfuscation scheme and benchmark combination. The relationship is linear as we report through a more fine-grained workload increase in Fig. 1. We analyse the energy consumption and execution time of code obfuscated by OLLVM and Tigress. Code obfuscated by Tigress generally consumes more energy and is slower than code obfuscated by OLLVM. This observation was consistent across other benchmark programs as well.

5   Security Analysis

Complexity of the obfuscated code is measured with respect to potency and resilience. We measure potency using metrics such as general software complexity and transform model and displayed in Table 3. Our results show that code obfuscated through tigress is more secure compared to OLLVM. As comparing transformations individually, control flow flattening has the highest score for both potency metrics. This is because control flow flattening transformation increases the depth of the code and thus increases the complexity of the obfuscated code.

Table 3. Comparison of potency measurement for OLLVM and Tigress. Here, F, B and I stand for Control Flow Flattening, Bogus Control Flow and Instruction Substitution.

	OLLVM		Tigress	
Transformation	General complexity	Transform model	General complexity	Transform model
FLA	2.54	0.782	2.99	0.98
BCF	2.42	0.714	2.90	0.82
SUB	2.01	0.23	2.42	0.41

Resilience measures the difficulty if the attacker is able to reverse engineer the obfuscated code. We measure resilience by deobfuscating the obfuscated code with use of a deobfuscation tool Jakstab. We conduct the experiment of deobfuscation for 30 min and analysed correctness, efficiency and time taken to complete the task and recorded the results in Table 4. Our results show that correctness for code obfuscated by tigress is zero and time taken for the task is 30 min. It is clear that within the time limit of the experiment conducted, it is difficult to deobfuscate the code obfuscated by tigress. However the code obfuscated by OLLVM is deobfuscated successfully and completed the task within 0.5 min. It is evident that the complexity introduced by tigress is higher as compared to OLLVM.

Table 4. Comparison of resilience measurement for OLLVM and Tigress. Execution time is measured in minutes. Here, F, B and I stands for Control Flow Flattening, Bogus Control Flow and Instruction Substitution

	OLLVM			Tigress		
Transformation	Correctness	Time	Efficiency	Correctness	Time	Efficiency
FLA	1	0.32	0.05	0	30	0
BCF	1	0.30	0.05	0	30	0
SUB	1	0.11	0.11	0	30	0

6   Analysis of Energy-Performance-Security Trade-Offs

Code obfuscation is the most popular technique to secure the source code from reverse engineering. Code obfuscation protect the code and simultaneously it causes negative impact on energy consumption. Software obfuscation on embedded devices is a challenge in terms of energy consumption. Thus it is necessary to balance the energy, performance and security of the obfuscated code.

We consider an application Dijkstra for the analysis. While analyzing the energy consumption for different transformation for OLLVM, energy consumption is increased by 44% for control flow flattening, 6.5% for bogus control flow and 4.6% for instruction substitution. In the case of tigress tool, energy consumption increases in a large scale as 96% for control flow flattening, 70% for bogus control flow and 60.9% for instruction substitution. As comparing the energy consumption of OLLVM and tigress, it is clear that Tigress consumes more energy of at most 18% for control flow flattening, 35% for bogus control flow and 1.85% for instruction substitution.

When we consider the results for security metrics, we realize that tigress provides more security than OLLVM. It was difficult for deobfuscation tool such as Jakstab to deobfuscate the code obfuscated by tigress tool as tigress impose more security features to avoid reverse engineering. Tigress provides protection by inserting anti-debugging tricks to avoid reverse engineering. The results of potency shows that control flow complexity is increased for tigress tool as it increases the depth of the source code. While analyzing the results of energy, performance and security, it is clear that increasing the security of the code consumes more energy and it affects it's performance.

Our results indicate that tigress obfuscation tool provides more security as compared to OLLVM and simultaneously increases energy consumption. Tigress provides protection by inserting anti-debugging tricks which are dependent on target platform and operating systems while OLLVM does not provide such protection as it is independent of target architecture. OLLVM tool provides security as well as consumes less energy. So it is better to choose obfuscator based on system capabilities and security requirements of applications. If application desires more security, then tigress can be utilized.

7   Discussion

We propose different methods to optimise the energy consumption and increase the performance of embedded applications. We propose to investigate the following as part of our future work.

Optimal Obfuscation
Obfuscation executive [27] determines the number and ordering of transformations. While applying more than one transformations, the order of applying the transformation is very important to produce an optimally obfuscated program. There are limitations in the order of applying transformations. A poor ordering of transformations can affect the obscurity and efficiency of the obfuscated code and it may affect the structure of the applications.

Application-Aware Obfuscation
It is evident from our results that tigress consumes more power than OLLVM and tigress also provide more secured obfuscated code. As considering the power-constraints and security of embedded applications, it is better to choose the tool and transformation based on the needs of the applications. If the application needs it's code to be secured, then developers can choose tigress tool as well as control flow flattening transformation. For the applications which is concerned about the power-constraints, it's is better to choose OLLVM tool.

8   Conclusion

Obfuscation is often looked as a monolithic program transformation to fortify code. However, there are several steps in obfuscation. These steps can be applied in arbitrary orders and combinations. In this paper, we showed that the configuration of the obfuscator and the combinations in which the transformations are applied has a large bearing on overall performance, energy consumption and security of the application. We discussed how the choice of the obfuscator has a bearing on non-functional performance of the application. Finally, our experiments revealed that application payload has an impact on the number of times a particular path is taken through a program and consequently, its energy consumption, performance and security. From our results, we have analysed energy-performance-security trade-offs. We expect our results to enable concerted efforts to develop tunable obfuscators based on system capabilities and security requirements of applications.

References

1. OLLVM Github. https://github.com/obfuscator-llvm/obfuscator
2. Lattner, C., Adve, V.: The LLVM compiler framework and infrastructure tutorial. In: Eigenmann, R., Li, Z., Midkiff, S.P. (eds.) LCPC 2004. LNCS, vol. 3602, pp. 15–16. Springer, Heidelberg (2005). https://doi.org/10.1007/11532378_2

3. Banescu, S., et al.: Code obfuscation against symbolic execution attacks. In: Proceedings of the 32nd Annual Conference on Computer Security Applications, ACSAC 2016, Los Angeles, CA, USA, 5–9 December 2016, pp. 189–200 (2016). http://dl.acm.org/citation.cfm?id=2991114

4. Behera, C.K., Bhaskari, D.L.: Different obfuscation techniques for code protection. Procedia Comput. Sci. **70**, 757–763 (2015)

5. Balakrishnan, A., Schulze, C.: Code obfuscation literature survey. CS701 Construction of compilers, 19 (2005)

6. Dong, S., et al.: Understanding android obfuscation techniques: a large-scale investigation in the wild. In: Beyah, R., Chang, B., Li, Y., Zhu, S. (eds.) SecureComm 2018. LNICST, vol. 254, pp. 172–192. Springer, Cham (2018). https://doi.org/10.1007/978-3-030-01701-9_10

7. Junod, P., et al.: Obfuscator-LLVM - software protection for the masses. In: Wyseur, B. (ed.) Proceedings of the IEEE/ACM 1st International Workshop on Software Protection, SPRO 2015, Firenze, Italy, 19 May 2015, pp. 3–9. IEEE. https://doi.org/10.1109/SPRO.2015.10

8. Piao, Y., Jung, J., Yi, J.H.: Structural and functional analyses of ProGuard obfuscation tool. J. Korean Inst. Commun. Inf. Sci. **38**(8), 654–662 (2013)

9. Allatori Java obfuscator. http://www.allatori.com/

10. Dasho - preemptive solutions. http://www.preemptive.com/products/dasho

11. Zelix klassmaster. http://www.zelix.com/klassmaster/

12. Joshi, H.P., Dhanasekaran, A., Dutta, R.: Trading off a vulnerability: does software obfuscation increase the risk of ROP attacks. J. Cyber Secur. Mobil. **4**(4), 305–324 (2015)

13. Scrinzi, F.: Behavioral analysis of obfuscated code. Master's thesis, University of Twente (2015)

14. Khan, S., et al.: Using predictive modeling for cross-program design space exploration in multicore systems. In: 16th International Conference on Parallel Architecture and Compilation Techniques (PACT 2007), pp. 327–338. IEEE (2007)

15. Sankaran, S.: Predictive modeling based power estimation for embedded multicore systems. In: Proceedings of the ACM International Conference on Computing Frontiers, pp. 370–375 (2016)

16. Sankaran, S., Sridhar, R.: Energy modeling for mobile devices using performance counters. In: 2013 IEEE 56th International Midwest Symposium on Circuits and Systems (MWSCAS), pp. 441–444. IEEE (2013)

17. Grech, N., et al.: Static energy consumption analysis of LLVM IR programs. Comput. Res. Repos., 1–12 (2014)

18. Ðuković, M., Varga, E.: Load profile-based efficiency metrics for code obfuscators. Acta Polytechnica Hungarica **12**(5) (2015)

19. Sankaran, S., Gupta, M.: Game theoretic modeling of power-performance trade-offs for mobile devices. In: 2018 8th International Symposium on Embedded Computing and System Design (ISED), pp. 220–224. IEEE (2018)

20. Sahin, C., et al.: How does code obfuscation impact energy usage? J. Softw. Evol. Process. **28**(7), 565–588 (2016)

21. Raj, A., Jithish, J., Sankaran, S.: Modelling the impact of code obfuscation on energy usage. In: DIAS/EDUDM@ ISEC (2017)

22. Viticchié, A., et al.: Assessment of source code obfuscation techniques. In: 2016 IEEE 16th International Working Conference on Source Code Analysis and Manipulation (SCAM), pp. 11–20. IEEE (2016)

23. Banescu, S., Collberg, C., Pretschner, A.: Predicting the resilience of obfuscated code against symbolic execution attacks via machine learning. In: 26th {USENIX} Security Symposium ({USENIX} Security 17), pp. 661–678 (2017)
24. Wu, Y., et al.: A framework for measuring the security of obfuscated software. In: Proceedings of 2010 International Conference on Test and Measurement (2010)
25. Powerstat. http://manpages.ubuntu.com/manpages/xenial/man8/powerstat.8. html
26. Guthaus, M.R., et al.: MiBench: a free, commercially representative embedded benchmark suite. In: Proceedings of the Fourth Annual IEEE International Workshop on Workload Characterization. WWC-4 (Cat. No. 01EX538), pp. 3–14. IEEE (2001)
27. Heffner, K., Collberg, C.: The obfuscation executive. In: Zhang, K., Zheng, Y. (eds.) ISC 2004. LNCS, vol. 3225, pp. 428–440. Springer, Heidelberg (2004). https://doi. org/10.1007/978-3-540-30144-8_36

Forward Secure Conjunctive-Keyword Searchable Symmetric Encryption Using Shamir Threshold Secret Sharing Scheme

Lin Li, Chungen Xu$^{(\boxtimes)}$, Zhongyi Liu, and Lin Mei

Nanjing University of Science and Technology, Nanjing 210094, China
{linli0923,xuchung,meilin}@njust.edu.cn, ZhongyiLiu950217@outlook.com

Abstract. Searchable symmetric encryption (SSE) has been widely applied in the encrypted database for queries in practice. Although SSE is powerful and feature-rich, it is always plagued by information leaks. Some recent attacks point out that forward security which disallows leakage from update operations, now becomes a basic requirement for any newly designed SSE schemes. Many forward secure searchable symmetric encryption (FSSE) schemes supporting single-keyword search have been proposed. Only a few SSE schemes can satisfy forward security and support conjunctive-keyword search at the same time, which are realized by adopting inefficient or complicated cryptographic tools. In this paper, we use an efficient cryptographic tool, Shamir threshold secret sharing scheme, to design an efficient and secure conjunctive-keyword FSSE scheme. Our scheme achieves sub-linear efficiency, and can easily be used in any single-keyword FSSE scheme to obtain a conjunctive-keyword FSSE scheme. Compared with the current conjunctive-keyword FSSE scheme, our scheme has a better update and search efficiency.

Keywords: Forward security · Conjunctive-keyword search · Shamir threshold secret sharing · Cloud computing

1 Introduction

With the development of network technology, cloud computing technology has been widely used by companies and individuals. While data users enjoy benefits such as low cost and ubiquitous access, data privacy becomes a major concern. To protect data privacy, data users usually encrypt data before uploading it to the untrusted storage server. However, encryption makes data incomprehensible, which results in common retrieval methods such as the keyword search cannot be directly executed on ciphertexts. Searchable symmetric encryption [14] provides the keyword search function while ensuring the security of cloud data. It allows a client to store encrypted data files on an untrusted server, then to retrieve all

Supported by National Natural Science Foundation of China (No: 62072240) and The National Key Research and Development Program of China (No. 2020YFB1804604).

© Springer Nature Singapore Pte Ltd. 2020
L. Batina and G. Li (Eds.): ATIS 2020, CCIS 1338, pp. 14–28, 2020.
https://doi.org/10.1007/978-981-33-4706-9_2

files containing a certain keyword by submitting a token that cryptographically encodes the keyword. Dynamic searchable symmetric encryption (DSSE) is more practical than SSE. It can support dynamic update operations. The user can add new files to the server or delete an old file in the server.

Some basic leakages are inevitable for SSE schemes as they support keyword search over encrypted data. Curtmola [4] proposed the definition of the leakage of access pattern and search pattern. DSSE schemes leak more information than SSE schemes. In DSSE schemes, an adversary can inject files containing some special keywords into the server's database. Then the adversary can use old search queries to search those injected files and then obtain some useful information from the search result. This kind of attack is called file injection attack (FIA) [20]. The FSSE schemes can well resist file injection attack. Because in an FSSE scheme, old queries cannot match the new file which was not queried before. Since 2016, several schemes have been proposed to achieve this goal using different cryptographic primitives, including Sophos [1] (uses trapdoor permutation (TDP)), Diana [2] (uses Constrained Pseudorandom Function (CPRF)), Dual [12] (uses keyed hash function), FSSE [19] (uses keyed-block chains), SGX-SE [17] (uses intel SGX) and VFSSE [7] (uses blockchain). In order to improve the practicability of FSSE scheme, some FSSE schemes that support conjunctive-keyword search have been proposed [8,18]. These schemes can search files containing multiple keywords. Most of the existing SSE schemes that support boolean queries leak the result pattern information [3]. This leakage allows the server to know which files contain part of the search keywords.

1.1 Our Contributions

The main contributions of this paper are as follows:

- We construct an efficient and secure FSSE scheme that supports conjunctive-keyword query using Shamir threshold scheme. Compared with the best current conjunctive-keyword FSSE scheme, our scheme has a better update and query efficiency.
- We give the security analysis and detailed efficiency description of our scheme. In addition, we implement our scheme using the Java programming language to test its practicality.

1.2 Related Work

Song et al. [14] proposed the first SSE scheme, which searching over the ciphertext instead of using the index table. So its search complexity is linear with the number of documents. After that, in order to improve search efficiency, many schemes using an index table [2,3,5,9,10,16] have been proposed. Goh et al. [5] proposed the first index-based SSE scheme. Schemes using index table will greatly improve search efficiency. In addition, researchers designed some SSE schemes with more properties, and hence, are more practical. Kamara et al. [10] proposed a DSSE scheme that can achieve sub-linear search efficiency. To support conjunctive-keyword search, Golle et al. [6] first proposed conjunctive-keyword search scheme. But their scheme is not very efficient. It has linear complexity with the whole number of documents. After that, Cash et al. [3] proposed the first SSE scheme that can achieve sub-linear search efficiency and support boolean queries. Lai [13] proposed a scheme that solves the Keyword-Pair Result Pattern leakage of OXT and achieves almost the same efficiency as OXT. But Lai's scheme needs one more round communication in search protocol. Zhang et al. [20] gave a formalized definition of a very strong attack, named file injection attack. This attack can easily recover the keyword of a query. Stefanov et al. [16] first formalized the notion of forward security for SSE scheme. After Bost [1] proposed a very creative way to design a practical FSSE scheme, many practical FSSE schemes were successively proposed. Song et al. [15] improved efficiency based on Bost's scheme using pseudo-random permutation. After that, Zhang et al. [21] proposed a more efficient way to construct FSSE scheme than Song's scheme. Recently, a few FSSE schemes support conjunctive-keyword search [8,18] were proposed. But the cryptographic tools they used are not efficient enough.

1.3   Organization

The rest of this paper is organized as follows. In Sect. 2, we describe the system model, threat model and design goals of our scheme. The notations and cryptographic primitives used in this paper are introduced in Sect. 3. In Sect. 4, we give the detailed structure of our scheme and describe how to deploy our scheme in a real scenario. We analyze the security of our scheme and compare the complexity with existing schemes and give the experiment results in Sects. 5 and 6, respectively. Finally, we give a brief conclusion in Sect. 7.

2   Problem Statement

2.1   System Model

There are three roles in our scheme: (1) the data owner, who encrypts data files and builds a searchable index before data outsourcing; (2) the data user, who issues search queries for interested keywords; (3) the server, who stores encrypted data files and responses the data user's search queries and the data owner's update queries. As illustrated in Fig. 1, the data owner encrypts data files and build a searchable index before data outsourcing. Upon receiving encrypted data files and the searchable index from the data owner, the server store them in the database. The data user uses the secret key, an interested keyword and the state of this keyword to issue search tokens. Afterwards, the server searches the index and returns the identities of data files containing the searched keyword. When the data owner performs update operations, for each keyword in W_{update}, he uses the secret key, this keyword and the state of this keyword to generate the update token. Then he uploads all update tokens and encrypted data files to the server.

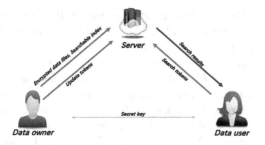

Fig. 1. System model

2.2 Threat Model

The server in our system is considered "honest-but-curious", that is to say, on the one hand, the server follows all the operations required by the system model; on the other hand, the adversary tries to deduce private information about the original data or searched keywords. Meanwhile, we suppose that the data owner and the data user are fully trusted.

2.3 Design Goals

We design our system with the following goals:

- **Forward Privacy:** Newly added files would not cause previous queries to leak information.
- **Update and Search Efficiency:** Our scheme is more efficient than other existing conjunctive-keyword FSSE schemes both in update and search efficiency.
- **Scalability:** The method we use to construct our scheme can be easily applied to other single-keyword FSSE schemes.

3 Cryptographic Background

In this section, we present some cryptographic primitives used in this paper.

3.1 Dynamic Symmetric Searchable Encryption

We briefly introduce DSSE based on [1]. A database $DB = (ind_i, W_i)_{i=1}^{D}$ is a tuple of index/keywords pairs with $ind_i \in \{0,1\}^l$, $W_i \in \{0,1\}^*$, where D is the number of documents in DB. $W = \bigcup_{i=1}^{D}$ denotes the total number of keywords in database DB. Let $N = \sum_{i=1}^{D} |W_i|$ be the number of document/keyword pairs. $DB(w)$ is the set of the document containing keyword w. Dynamic searchable encryption can be denoted by $\Pi = (Setup, Search, Update)$. Among them, $Setup$ is an algorithm, $Search$ and $Update$ are two protocols between server and client. Π can be described as follows:

- *Setup(DB)* is used to initialize and start a system. It takes as input a plaintext database DB, and outputs (EDB, K, σ). EDB is the encrypted database, K is the secret key and σ is client's state.
- *Search(EDB, K, q, σ)* is a protocol between the server and the user. The user first uses his secret key K, state σ and a search query $q = \{w_1, \cdots, w_l\}$ to generate a search token, then he sends the token to the server. Server runs the match algorithm which takes as input search token and its encrypted database EDB, then sends back the search result to the client.
- *Update(EDB, K, σ, op, in)* $= (Update_C(K, \sigma, op, in), Update_S(EDB))$ is a protocol between the user and the server. $Update_C$ is run by the user. The $Update_C$ takes as input the key K, state σ, operation op and input in parsed as the index ind and a set of keywords W_{ind} and output a update token. The $Update_S$ is run by the server and takes as input EDB. The operation op is taken from the set $\{add, del\}$, meaning the addition and deletion operations of a document/keyword pair.

3.2   Pseudo-Random Functions and Permutations

In addition to encryption schemes, we also make use of pseudo-random functions (PRF) and permutations (PRP), which are polynomial-time computable functions that cannot be distinguished from random functions by any probabilistic polynomial-time adversary. We refer the reader to [11] for formal definitions of CPA-security PRFs and PRPs.

3.3   Shamir Threshold Secret Sharing Scheme

The Shamir threshold secret sharing scheme can denote by $\Pi = \{$Setup, Distribute, Decrypt$\}$. For a (t, n) threshold scheme, it can be briefly described as follows:

- **Setup**. Secret distributor D randomly selects n elements $\{x_1, \cdots, x_n\}$ where $x_j \in \mathcal{Z}_p$.
- **Distribute**. For the secret message $S \in \mathcal{Z}_p$, D randomly selects a polynomial function $p(x) \xleftarrow{\$} F_p[x]$ and then let $p(0) = S$. Then D computes sub-secret messages $\{s_1, \cdots, s_n\}$ where $s_i = p(x_i)$. Then D distributes (x_i, s_i) to n secret holders respectively.
- **Decrypt**. At least t secret holders are required to decrypt the secret information S. As long as at least t pairs (x_i, s_i) are obtained, we can use the Lagrange interpolation formula to decrypt the secret information:

$$S = p(0) = \sum_{i=1}^{t} (s_i \cdot \prod_{j=1, j \neq i}^{t} \frac{-x_j}{x_i - x_j}).$$

4 Our Proposed Scheme: FSSE Scheme Using Shamir Threshold Secret Sharing Scheme

In this section, we are going to introduce our scheme in details. In our scheme, we use the Shamir threshold secret sharing scheme to support conjunctive-keyword search. We denote W as an ordered keyword space which is not necessary to keep confidentially, i.e., the server can access W. Let N be the cardinality of the ordered keyword space W, i.e., $N = |W|$. We also employ two hash functions H_1, H_2, two pseudo-random functions F, F_p and a pseudo-random permutation PRP in our scheme:

$$H_1 : \{0,1\}^* \rightarrow \{0,1\}^\lambda, \ H_2 : \{0,1\}^* \rightarrow \{0,1\}^{2\lambda+1}$$
$$F : \{0,1\}^\lambda \times \{0,1\}^* \rightarrow \{0,1\}^\lambda, \ F_p : \{0,1\}^\lambda \times \{0,1\}^* \rightarrow \mathbb{Z}_p$$
$$PRP : \{0,1\}^\lambda \times \{1,...,N\} \rightarrow \{1,...,N\}$$

Besides, we need to predefine a threshold t for Shamir threshold secret sharing scheme. Let $l = |W_{ind}|$ and $m = |W_{search}|$. We assume that l and m are both integral multiples of t. The handling of other situations will be introduced later in Subsect. 4.2.

4.1 Construction

As can be seen from Fig. 2, our scheme contains three protocols: *Setup, Update* and *Search*. The protocols can be described as follows:

– *Setup*(1^λ). This is a protocol between the data owner and the server. The data owner simply chooses a random λ-bit string as the secret key k_s and initializes an empty map Σ. Following most of the existing settings, the secret key k_s in this paper is assumed to be transferred via a secure channel between the data owner and the data user. As for the server, it initializes an empty map T.

– *Update*($ind, (w_{t_1}, \cdots, w_{t_l}), k_s, \Sigma, T$). This is also a protocol between the data owner and server. When the data owner wants to update (add or delete) a file ind containing keywords W_{ind}, for each keyword $w_i \in W_{ind}$, he generates t_w, st_{c+1}, e and u. Then he runs the following step to generate the vector C. He randomly generates a polynomial function $p(x) \in F_p[x]$ where $p(0) = 0$ and the degree of $p(x)$ is $t - 1$. Then he computes the secret message S and set $Ploy(x) = p(x) + S$. For each $j \in \{t_1, \cdots, t_l\}$, the data owner computes $x_j = F_p(k_s, w_j)$ and $y_j = Ploy(x_j)$. To achieve random assignment, we use a pseudo-random permutation PRP to permute the sequence $(1, 2, ..., N)$ which is on behalf of the position of keyword. He computes $K_{permute} = F(k_s, 0)$ and $pos = PRP(K_{permute}, j)$, then sets $C[pos]$ to y_j. The other elements of C are set to be random values. Finally, the data owner sends the update token (u, e, C) to the server and then deletes the polynomial function $Ploy(x)$. After receiving the update token (u, e, C), the server put it in to the map T, i.e., $T[u] = (e, C)$.

$Setup(1^\lambda)$

Data owner:

1: $k_s \xleftarrow{\$} \{0,1\}^\lambda$
2: initialize an empty map Σ

Server:

3: initialize an empty map T

$Update(ind, (w_{t_1}, w_{t_2}, \cdots, w_{t_l}), k_s, \Sigma, T)$

Data owner:

1: **for** $j \in \{t_1, \cdots, t_l\}$ **do**
2:    $x_j \leftarrow F_p(k_s, w_j)$
3: **end for**
4: **for** $i \in \{t_1, \cdots, t_l\}$ **do**
5:    $t_w \leftarrow F(k_s, w_i)$
6:    $st_c \leftarrow \Sigma[w_i]$
7:    **if** $st_c = \perp$ **then**
8:       $st_1 \xleftarrow{\$} \{0,1\}^\lambda$
9:       $e \leftarrow H_2(t_w || st_1) \oplus (\perp || op || ind)$
10:    **else**
11:       $st_{c+1} \xleftarrow{\$} \{0,1\}^{\lambda'}$
12:       $e \leftarrow H_2(t_w || st_{c+1}) \oplus (st_c || op || ind)$
13:    **end if**
14:    $\Sigma[w_i] \leftarrow st_{c+1}$
15:    $u \leftarrow H_1(t_w || st_{c+1})$
16:    $C \leftarrow 0$ where $C \in \mathbb{Z}_p^N$
17:    $S \leftarrow F_p(t_w, st_{c+1})$
18:    $p(x) \leftarrow PloyGen()$
19:    $Ploy(x) \leftarrow p(x) + S$
20:    $K_{permute} \leftarrow F(k_s, 0)$
21:    **for** $1 \leq j \leq N$ **do**
22:       **if** $j \in \{t_1, \cdots, t_l\}$ **then**
23:          $y_j \leftarrow Ploy(x_j)$
24:          $pos = PRP(K_{permute}, j)$
25:          $C[pos] \leftarrow y_j$
26:       **end if**
27:    **end for**
28:    **for** $1 \leq j \leq N$ **do**
29:       **if** $C[j] = 0$ **then**
30:          $x_j \xleftarrow{\$} \mathbb{Z}_p$
31:          $y_j \leftarrow Ploy(x_j)$
32:          $C[j] \leftarrow y_j$
33:       **end if**
34:    **end for**

35:    send (u, e, C) to the server
36: **end for**

Server:

37: $T[u] \leftarrow (e, C)$

$Search((w_{t_1} \wedge w_{t_2} \wedge \cdots \wedge w_{t_m}), k_s, \Sigma, T)$

Data user:

1: $st_c \leftarrow \Sigma[w_{t_1}]$
2: **if** $st_c = \perp$ **then**
3:    **return** ϕ
4: **end if**
5: $t_w \leftarrow F(k_s, w_{t_1})$
6: $K_{permute} \leftarrow F(k_s, 0)$
7: initialize an empty set Q
8: **for** $j \in \{t_1, \cdots, t_m\}$ **do**
9:    $x_j \leftarrow F_p(k_s, w_j)$
10:    $pos = PRP(K_{permute}, j)$
11:    $Q \leftarrow Q \cup (pos, x_j)$
12: **end for**
13: send (t_w, st_c, Q) to the server

Server:

14: initialize two empty set R, Δ
15: **while** $st_c \neq \perp$ **do**
16:    $u \leftarrow H_1(t_w || st_c)$
17:    $(e, C) \leftarrow T[u]$
18:    initialize an empty coordinate set $\mathcal{D}$
19:    **for** $(pos, x_j) \in Q$ **do**
20:       add $(x_j, C[pos])$ to $\mathcal{D}$
21:    **end for**
22:    $(st_{c-1}, op, ind) \leftarrow H_2(t_w || st_c) \oplus e$
23:    **if** $op = del$ **then**
24:       $\Delta = \Delta \cup \{ind\}$
25:    **else**
26:       **if** $ind \in \Delta$ **then**
27:          $\Delta = \Delta \setminus \{ind\}$
28:       **else**
29:          $S \leftarrow F_p(t_w, st_c)$
30:          $test \leftarrow Scan(\mathcal{D}, S)$
31:          **if** $test = true$ **then**
32:             $R \leftarrow R \cup \{ind\}$
33:          **end if**
34:       **end if**
35:    **end if**
36: **end while**
37: send R to data user

Fig. 2. Forward secure conjunctive-keyword searchable symmetric encryption using Shamir threshold secret sharing scheme

– $Search((w_{t_1} \wedge \cdots \wedge w_{t_m}), k_s, \Sigma, T)$. This is a protocol between the data user and the server. When the data user wants to search the files containing keywords $W_{search} = (w_{t_1}, \cdots, w_{t_m})$, he first looks up the map Σ to determine if there is any document containing keywords w_{t_1}. If exiting (i.e., $st_c \neq \perp$), the data user computes t_w and initializes a set Q. For each $j \in \{t_1, \cdots, t_m\}$, he also computes $K_{permute} = F(k_s, 0)$ and $pos = PRP(K_{permute}, j)$. Then he gets $x_j = F_p(k_s, w_j)$ and puts (pos, x_j) into Q. And then the data user sends the search token (st_c, t_w, Q) to the server. After receiving the search token, the server can iterate over the entire chain associated with w_{t_1}. In each iteration, the server can combine x_j with y_j who are in the same position to form a coordinate set $\mathcal{D}$. After getting the coordinate set $\mathcal{D}$, the server runs the test program $Scan(\mathcal{D}, S)$ and get test result $test$. If $test$ is true, the server puts the file ind in R. Finally, the server sends back the result set R to the user.

The test program $Scan(\mathcal{D}, S)$ can be described as follows: First, it groups the coordinates in $\mathcal{D}$ according to threshold t. Later, in the Subsect. 4.2, we will discuss how to deal with the situation when the number of coordinates in $\mathcal{D}$ is not an integral multiple of t. Second, for each group, it runs the decryption algorithm of Shamir threshold scheme and then gets a message S'. If $S' \neq S$, it returns $false$, otherwise tests the next group. If all groups pass the test, it returns $true$.

4.2 How to Deploy

In this subsection, we are going to analyze what we should pay attention to when actually deploying this scheme.

– **How to deal with the situations when the number of search keywords is not an integral multiple of the threshold t.** As described in the construction, the test program $Scan(\mathcal{D}, S)$ can deal with the situation when the number of coordinates in $\mathcal{D}$ is an integral multiple of t. There are two other situations: (1) after grouping according to the threshold t(there is at least one group), the remaining coordinates are not enough for one group. In this situation, it randomly selects the coordinates of previous groups to supplement to the length of t. (2) the number of coordinates in $\mathcal{D}$ is less than the threshold t. To deal with this situation, we need to reserve $t - 1$ positions in the predefined keyword space W to store $t - 1$ virtual keywords. For example, these virtual keywords can be described as $virtual_1, virtual_2, ..., virtual_{t-1}$. In this way, the predefined keyword space W can be written as $(virtual_1, virtual_2, ..., virtual_{t-1}, w_t, w_{t+1}, ..., w_{|W|})$. We assume that every data file contains all these virtual keywords. These virtual keywords are treated as real keywords when update and search protocols are performed. In this way, we can make sure that there is at least one group in the situation (1).

– **How to choose threshold t.** In this paper, We construct a conjunctive-keyword FSSE scheme using the Shamir threshold scheme. The threshold of Shamir threshold scheme is not necessary to be very large. If the threshold t is large, we need to predefine too many virtual keywords in the keyword space W. Therefore, in our scheme, we set t to 5 reasonably.

5 Security Analysis

In this section, we analyze the security of our scheme. Informally, the security of our scheme depends on the security of the hash function, pseudo-random function and Shamir threshold scheme. To support conjunctive-keyword search, we add an extra ciphertext into the update token, and then the server can do a conjunctive-keyword search on the encrypted database. So as long as this extra ciphertext does not leak any information about the keywords of the newly added file, our scheme can guarantee forward security. Let $W_{ind} = \{w_{t_1}, \cdots, w_{t_l}\}$ be the keywords in a file ind, and $W_{search} = \{w_{t_1}, \cdots, w_{t_m}\}$ be the keywords in a search query. For a search query q, data user uses w_{t_1} to get t_w and st_c. We call this kind of keyword as a $stag$. For a search query q, let $stag = Stag(q)$. Let $Hist = \{(DB_i, q_i)\}_{i=0}^{Q}$, where q_i is an update query or search query, DB_i is a snapshot of the database DB. For a search query W_{search}, let $W_s = \{w_i | w_i \in W_{search}, w_i \in W_{ind}\}$. Before we define the leakage functions, we provide some additional functions that will be necessary in the definition of leakage functions as follows:

- Search Pattern:

$$sp(w_{t_1}) = \{i | Stag(q_i) = w_{t_1}, q_i \in Hist\}.$$

- Update History:

$$uh(w_{t_1}) = \{(i, op, ind_i) | q_i \text{ is a search query}, Stag(q_i) = w_{t_1}\}.$$

- Result Pattern:

$$RP(W_{search}) = \{SKRP(W_{search}), KPRP(W_{search}), IP(W_{search})\}.$$

With the help of all above descriptions, we define the leakage functions in our scheme as follows:

$$\mathcal{L}_{Setup} = \bot$$
$$\mathcal{L}_{Search}(W_{search}) = (sp(w_{t_1}), uh(w_{t_1}), RP(W_{search}))$$
$$\mathcal{L}_{Update}(i, op_i, W_{ind_i}, ind_i) = (i, op_i, ind_i)$$

We are now ready to state the following theorem regarding the security of our scheme.

Theorem 1. *If H_2, H_3, F, F_p and Shamir threshold scheme are secure cryptographic primitives, then our scheme is an $\mathcal{L} - adaptively - secure$ SSE scheme with $\mathcal{L} = (\mathcal{L}_{Setup}, \mathcal{L}_{Search}, \mathcal{L}_{Update})$.*

Proof. We briefly describe the proof of our scheme based on [15] and [8]. We are going to design four games and one simulator. Then we prove the $\mathbf{Real}_{\mathcal{A}}^{\Pi}(\lambda)$ and game G_4 are indistinguishable, and G_4 and $\mathbf{Ideal}_{\mathcal{A},\mathcal{S}}^{\Pi}(\lambda)$ are indistinguishable. Then $\mathbf{Real}_{\mathcal{A}}^{\Pi}(\lambda)$ and $\mathbf{Ideal}_{\mathcal{A},\mathcal{S}}^{\Pi}(\lambda)$ are indistinguishable. These games and simulator can be briefly described as follows:

Game G_1: G_1 is the same as $\mathbf{Real}_{\mathcal{A}}^{\Pi}(\lambda)$ except that the pseudo-random functions F and F_p. The experiment maintains two maps instead of using F and F_p.

The experiment randomly generates values for each different input and records it in the corresponding map. According to the properties of pseudo-random function, $\mathbf{Real}_{\mathcal{A}}^{\Pi}(\lambda)$ and G_1 are indistinguishable.

Game G_2: Compared to G_1, a random oracle $\mathbf{H}_1$ is used to replace the hash function H_1, and a map $\mathbf{MH}_1$ is used to store the values of the hash function H_1. Similar to the game G_2 described in [15], the values in this map have the property of delayed exposure, i.e. The values of H_1 in $\mathbf{MH}_1$ are not exposed to the oracle $\mathbf{H}_1$ immediately. For example, if the state st_c has been submitted to the server, the random oracle will return the value correctly, otherwise the random oracle will return a random value. According to the properties of a hash function, G_2 and G_1 are indistinguishable.

Game G_3: Based on G_2, G_3 replaces the hash function H_2 with a random oracle $\mathbf{H}_2$. And a map $\mathbf{MH}_2$ is maintained by the experiment to store the value of H_2. $\mathbf{H}_2$ has the same properties as the random oracle $\mathbf{H}_1$. According to the properties of hash function, G_3 and G_2 are indistinguishable.

Game G_4: The main difference between G_3 and G_4 is the way the update token and search token are generated. In the update protocol, the u, e and x_j are random values. In the search protocol, t_W, st_c and Q are generated on the fly, i.e. the experiment queries the maps maintained by itself to generate the search token, and expose the values $\mathbf{H}_2(t_w\|st_i)$ and $\mathbf{H}_1(t_w\|st_c)$ to the adversary. Then G_4 and G_3 are indistinguishable.

$\mathbf{Ideal}_{\mathcal{A},\mathcal{S}}^{\Pi}(\lambda)$: Compared to G_4, $\mathbf{Ideal}_{\mathcal{A},\mathcal{S}}^{\Pi}(\lambda)$ replaces the algorithms *Shamir.Setup*, *Shamir.Distribute* and *Shamir.Decrypt* with three simulators: *Shamir.S_{Setup}*, *Shamir.$S_{Distribute}$* and *Shamir.$S_{Decrypt}$*. The adversary cannot distinguish between Shamir threshold scheme and these simulators in polynomial time. Then $\mathbf{Ideal}_{\mathcal{A},\mathcal{S}}^{\Pi}(\lambda)$ and G_4 are indistinguishable. Finally, we prove the $\mathbf{Ideal}_{\mathcal{A},\mathcal{S}}^{\Pi}(\lambda)$ and $\mathbf{Real}_{\mathcal{A}}^{\Pi}(\lambda)$ are indistinguishable.

6   Performance Evaluation

In this section, we will compare the complexity of our scheme with two existing conjunctive-keyword FSSE schemes Hu's scheme [8] and FOXT-B scheme [18], and then code programs to compare the efficiency of three schemes.

6.1   Complexity Comparison

Table 1 demonstrates the comparison of communication complexity in Hu's scheme [8], FOXT-B [18] and our scheme. As can be seen from Table 1, the update token of FOXT-B is independent of N, and the update tokens in Hu's scheme and our scheme are all linear with N, but ours is smaller than Hu's. In terms of search token, our scheme has the shorter search token than the other two schemes.

Table 1. Comparison of communication complexity. N is the size of the predefined keyword space W, $|\mathbb{G}_1|$ is the bit size of the element of $\mathbb{G}_1$, $|\mathbb{Z}_p|$ is the bit size of the element of $\mathbb{Z}_p$, m is the number of keywords in a search query, i.e., $m = |W_{search}|$, c is the average size of $DB(w)$ and λ is the security parameter.

Scheme	Update token	Search token
Hu's scheme [8]	$(N+1) \cdot |\mathbb{G}_1| + 2\lambda$	$2(\lambda + |\mathbb{Z}_p|) + (N+1)|\mathbb{G}_1|$
FOXT-B [18]	$2\lambda + |\mathbb{Z}_p| + |\mathbb{G}_1|$	$2\lambda + |\mathbb{Z}_p| + c(m-1)|\mathbb{G}_1|$
Our scheme	$3\lambda + 1 + N \cdot |\mathbb{Z}_p|$	$2\lambda + m(|\mathbb{Z}_p| + logN)$

Table 2 shows the comparison of computational complexity in Hu's scheme, FOXT-B and our scheme. As for the computation of the data owner in the update protocol, our scheme is more efficient than Hu's scheme and FOXT-B. The reason is that we use hash functions, polynomial generation and polynomial computation in our scheme, which are all efficient cryptographic primitives. Compared with our scheme, Hu's scheme and FOXT-B use IPE.*Encrypt* and the trapdoor permutation, respectively. They both require high computational overhead.

In terms of the computation of the data owner in the search protocol, our scheme is also more efficient than Hu's scheme and FOXT-B. Our scheme just use hash functions, pseudo-random functions and permutation. The high computational overhead in Hu's scheme and FOXT-B is due to the exponentiation operation in cyclic group $\mathbb{G}_1$ and $\mathbb{G}_t$.

In the aspect of the computation of the server in the search protocol, our scheme is also more efficient than Hu's scheme and FOXT-B. The reason is similar to the above comparison, the efficiency of Shamir.Decrypt is much higher than IPE.Decrypt and the trapdoor permutation.

Table 2. Comparison of computational complexity. N is the size of the predefined keyword space W, H is the computation cost of hash function and pseudo-random function, π is the computation cost of trapdoor permutation function, c is the average size of $DB(w)$, m is the number of keywords in a search query, i.e. $m = |W_{search}|$ and l is the number of keywords in one file, i.e. $l = |W_{ind}|$. E is the computation cost of an exponentiation operation in cyclic group $\mathbb{G}_1$ and $\mathbb{G}_t$. $I.E$, $I.K$ and $I.D$ are the computation cost of $IPE.Encrypt$, $IPE.KeyGen$ and $IPE.Decrypt$, respectively. PG and P are the computation cost of PolyGen and Ploy in the update protocol, respectively. S.D is the computation cost of $Decrypt$ of the Shamir threshold scheme.

Scheme	Update.data owner	Search.data owner	Search.server
Hu's scheme [8]	$l(4H + \pi) + I.E$	$H + I.K$	$c(3H + \pi + I.D)$
FOXT-B [18]	$l(5H + \pi + E)$	$H + c(m-1)E$	$c(H + m \cdot E + \pi)$
Our scheme	$l(6+l)H + PG + lNP$	$2(m+1)H$	$c(3H + \lfloor m/t \rfloor S.D)$

6.2   Experiment Results

In this subsection, we use a set of data to test the efficiency of search and update protocol in our scheme. We run the program on a personal computer with Windows10 OS, Intel(R) Core(TM) i7-9750H CPU 2.60 GHz, and 8 GB of DDR4 RAM. We use the JPBC library and choose the type A pairing to implement the pairing function. Let $\lambda = 256$ be the security parameter. We choose SM3 as a pseudo-random permutation, hash functions and pseudo-random functions. Besides, we set N to 1000 in our scheme, that is, the predefined keyword space W has 1000 keywords. According to the complexity comparison, l, m and c are the main factors affecting the efficiency of update and search protocol. So we test how the efficiency change with these variables.

Note that the running time of Hu's scheme is much larger than our scheme and FOXT-B because Hu's scheme performs the XOR operation many times, i.e., the XOR operation on the ciphertext of IPE. In fact, running per XOR operation on the ciphertext of IPE will take 20 ms on our personal computer. If we set N to 1000, the computation cost will reach 20000 ms, which is unacceptable in practice. So we only give the comparison result of our scheme and FOXT-B.

In the update protocol, l, i.e., the number of keywords in an update file, is the main factor affecting efficiency. Therefore, we vary l from 10 to 100 to test the execution time of the update protocol. As shown in Fig. 3, similar to FOXT-B, the execution time of update protocol in our scheme is linear with l. But the execution time of our scheme is a little longer than FOXT-B. In fact, the number of keywords in a file usually does not exceed 50. Therefore, the difference between the cost of update in two schemes can be accepted. And we find that when the number of keywords is 50, the cost of our scheme is about 21 ms. Actually, our scheme has a good efficiency. Later, we will see that our scheme has a much larger improvement than FOXT-B in the search protocol.

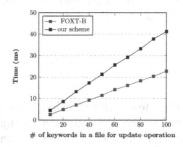

Fig. 3. The efficiency of update protocol

In terms of the execution time in the search protocol, m and c are the main factors affecting the search protocol's efficiency. Therefore, we test how the efficiency change with these two variables. As we can see from Fig. 4, the left picture shows how the execution time changes with m, i.e., the number of keywords in a search query. In this test, we fix c at 100. As for FOXT-B, its cost is linear with m. However, our scheme's cost is zigzag due to the Shamir threshold t (we set t to 5 in our scheme). As we have discussed in Subsect. 4.2, if the coordinates are not enough for one group after grouping, the search protocol randomly selects the coordinates of previous groups to supplement the length to t. As a result, the cost of $t+1$ keywords query is almost the same as $t+2$ keywords query. At last, we can find that our scheme has a much better performance than FOXT-B. It can be seen from Fig. 4 that the difference in the execution time is about 60 ms when m is equal to 25. And this difference is going to increase rapidly as m increases.

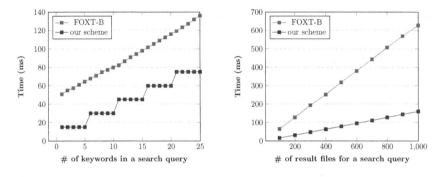

Fig. 4. The efficiency of search protocol

The right picture of Fig. 4 shows how the execution time changes with c, i.e., the number of result files for a search query. Similar to F0XT-B, the execution time of our scheme is linear with c. But there is a big gap between the growth rates of our scheme and FOXT-B. When c is equal to 1000, the difference between the two schemes is about 430 ms. And this difference is going to increase rapidly as c increases.

7   Conclusion

In this paper, we analyze the feasibility of using Shamir threshold scheme to support conjunctive-keyword search and construct a conjunctive-keyword FSSE scheme with the help of Shamir threshold scheme. We analyze the security and efficiency of our scheme and how to deploy our scheme in the real scenario. Compared with the existing conjunctive-keyword FSSE scheme, our scheme is more efficient and practical.

References

1. Bost, R.: $\sum o\varphi o\varsigma$: forward secure searchable encryption. In: Weippl, E.R., Katzenbeisser, S., Kruegel, C., Myers, A.C., Halevi, S. (eds.) Proceedings of the 2016 ACM SIGSAC Conference on Computer and Communications Security, Vienna, Austria, 24–28 October 2016, pp. 1143–1154. ACM (2016)
2. Bost, R., Minaud, B., Ohrimenko, O.: Forward and backward private searchable encryption from constrained cryptographic primitives. In: Proceedings of the 2017 ACM SIGSAC Conference on Computer and Communications Security, pp. 1465–1482 (2017)
3. Cash, D., Jarecki, S., Jutla, C., Krawczyk, H., Roşu, M.-C., Steiner, M.: Highly-scalable searchable symmetric encryption with support for Boolean queries. In: Canetti, R., Garay, J.A. (eds.) CRYPTO 2013. LNCS, vol. 8042, pp. 353–373. Springer, Heidelberg (2013). https://doi.org/10.1007/978-3-642-40041-4_20
4. Curtmola, R., Garay, J., Kamara, S., Ostrovsky, R.: Searchable symmetric encryption: improved definitions and efficient constructions. J. Comput. Secur. **19**(5), 895–934 (2011)
5. Goh, E.J., et al.: Secure indexes. IACR Cryptology ePrint Archive 2003, 216 (2003)
6. Golle, P., Staddon, J., Waters, B.: Secure conjunctive keyword search over encrypted data. In: Jakobsson, M., Yung, M., Zhou, J. (eds.) ACNS 2004. LNCS, vol. 3089, pp. 31–45. Springer, Heidelberg (2004). https://doi.org/10.1007/978-3-540-24852-1_3
7. Guo, Y., Zhang, C., Jia, X.: Verifiable and forward-secure encrypted search using blockchain techniques. In: 2020 IEEE International Conference on Communications, ICC 2020, Dublin, Ireland, 7–11 June 2020, pp. 1–7. IEEE (2020)
8. Hu, C., et al.: Forward secure conjunctive-keyword searchable encryption. IEEE Access **7**, 35035–35048 (2019)
9. Kamara, S., Papamanthou, C.: Parallel and dynamic searchable symmetric encryption. In: Sadeghi, A.-R. (ed.) FC 2013. LNCS, vol. 7859, pp. 258–274. Springer, Heidelberg (2013). https://doi.org/10.1007/978-3-642-39884-1_22
10. Kamara, S., Papamanthou, C., Roeder, T.: Dynamic searchable symmetric encryption. In: Proceedings of the 2012 ACM Conference on Computer and Communications Security, pp. 965–976 (2012)
11. Katz, J., Lindell, Y.: Introduction to Modern Cryptography, 2nd edn. CRC Press, Boca Raton (2014)
12. Kim, K.S., Kim, M., Lee, D., Park, J.H., Kim, W.: Forward secure dynamic searchable symmetric encryption with efficient updates. In: Thuraisingham, B.M., Evans, D., Malkin, T., Xu, D. (eds.) Proceedings of the 2017 ACM SIGSAC Conference on Computer and Communications Security, CCS 2017, Dallas, TX, USA, 30 October–03 November 2017, pp. 1449–1463. ACM (2017)
13. Lai, S., et al.: Result pattern hiding searchable encryption for conjunctive queries. In: Proceedings of the 2018 ACM SIGSAC Conference on Computer and Communications Security, pp. 745–762 (2018)
14. Song, D.X., Wagner, D., Perrig, A.: Practical techniques for searches on encrypted data. In: Proceeding 2000 IEEE Symposium on Security and Privacy, S&P 2000, pp. 44–55. IEEE (2000)
15. Song, X., Dong, C., Yuan, D., Xu, Q., Zhao, M.: Forward private searchable symmetric encryption with optimized I/O efficiency. IEEE Trans. Dependable Secure Comput. **17**, 912–927 (2018)

16. Stefanov, E., Papamanthou, C., Shi, E.: Practical dynamic searchable encryption with small leakage. In: NDSS, vol. 71, pp. 72–75 (2014)
17. Vo, V., Lai, S., Yuan, X., Sun, S., Nepal, S., Liu, J.K.: Accelerating forward and backward private searchable encryption using trusted execution. CoRR abs/2001.03743 (2020)
18. Wang, Y., Wang, J., Sun, S., Miao, M., Chen, X.: Toward forward secure sse supporting conjunctive keyword search. IEEE Access **7**, 142762–142772 (2019)
19. Wei, Y., Lv, S., Guo, X., Liu, Z., Huang, Y., Li, B.: FSSE: forward secure searchable encryption with keyed-block chains. Inf. Sci. **500**, 113–126 (2019)
20. Zhang, Y., Katz, J., Papamanthou, C.: All your queries are belong to us: The power of file-injection attacks on searchable encryption. In: 25th {USENIX} Security Symposium ({USENIX} Security 16), pp. 707–720 (2016)
21. Zhang, Z., Wang, J., Wang, Y., Su, Y., Chen, X.: Towards efficient verifiable forward secure searchable symmetric encryption. In: Sako, K., Schneider, S., Ryan, P.Y.A. (eds.) ESORICS 2019. LNCS, vol. 11736, pp. 304–321. Springer, Cham (2019). https://doi.org/10.1007/978-3-030-29962-0_15

Digital Forensics for Drones: A Study of Tools and Techniques

Sowmya Viswanathan[1] and Zubair Baig[1,2(✉)]

[1] School of Information Technology, Deakin University, Geelong, VIC 3216, Australia
{sviswanathan,zubair.baig}@deakin.edu.au
[2] Centre for Cyber Security Research and Innovation (CSRI), Deakin University, Geelong, VIC 3216, Australia

Abstract. Digital forensics investigation on drones has gained significant popularity during the recent past mainly due to intensifying drone-related cybercrime activities. Collecting valid digital evidence from confiscated drones and to prove a case in the court of law has been a difficult and lengthy process due to various factors including choice of tools. Consequently, to simplify and speed up the investigation process, the most apt forensic investigation tools must be selected to carry out the investigation, accompanied with data mining techniques for data analysis and visualization, ascertains accuracy in reporting. We present our findings on tool selection and intelligent clustering of DJI Mavic Air drone data. The proposed methodology can help forensic investigators identify the most pertinent forensic investigation tools to foster a sound artificial intelligence-based forensic investigation process. Experiments were conducted on sample drone data, with findings reported on the superiority of Airdata.com and Autopsy forensic tools over others.

Keywords: Drones · DJI Mavic Air · Digital forensics tools · Self-Organizing Map (SOM)

1 Introduction

Drones, also known as UAVs (Unmanned Aerial Vehicles), are pilotless aircrafts that are operated remotely and have increasing use for both civilian as well as military applications [2]. Drones comprise various components including high performance cameras, GPS, and an on-device SD card for storing recorded videos and images, which can be subsequently unmounted for processing and analysis of data [15]. In the report (Business Insider, 2019), it is stated that drones can be flown for various applications including for aerial photography, delivery of services and inspections/surveillance. The above-mentioned uses of UAVs are becoming very common in recent days due to the rapid advances in drone technology and its usage is relevant in tracking locations and in inaccessible locations, such as rainforests and caves.

Despite the advantages of flying a drone, they are increasingly being involved in cyber-attacks [12]. Moreover, the reliance of drone technology on vulnerable standards

© Springer Nature Singapore Pte Ltd. 2020
L. Batina and G. Li (Eds.): ATIS 2020, CCIS 1338, pp. 29–41, 2020.
https://doi.org/10.1007/978-981-33-4706-9_3

such as IEEE 802.11, expose them to a range of security threats; as the drone and ground station controller typically communicate through the Wi-Fi standard. It is therefore essential to assess the security and privacy concerns appertaining to drone usage. Further challenges are posed due to the capability of drones to capture data over extended time periods owing to significant advances in sensor technology [1]. For example, it can not only capture images and videos, but it can also capture radio signals, gas emission, geodetic data in binary format, albeit the capacity to capture information highly depends on its storage limitations and software downtime. The ability to record videos and monitor human movement either knowingly or unknowingly plays against basic tenets of civil liberty, increasing privacy-related concerns and exposing the information to the adversary, for potential misuse [29]. During the investigation process, the drone, which is captured from the crime location, may contain a lot of data comprising on-board sensory data, flight paths, audio and video; which can be extracted using forensic tools to identify the criminal trait. Investigating flight data and managing the multi-platform nature of drones can be a big challenge in the investigation process [7]. Moreover, forensic investigation tools have been traditionally designed for various computer forensic activities including; network, device, mobile platforms, databases, memory and email forensics. Each of these domains uses a different set of tools to acquire and examine the data obtained from the device [10]. In this paper, we focus on identifying effective forensics tools, where we present the extraction and identification of important artefacts from the DJI Mavic Air drone images obtained from the CFReDS project [21]. Our experiments were based on [15] in terms of the digital investigation process, utilising intelligent clustering Self- Organizing Maps (SOM) algorithm for clustering the acquired drone data and to trace the criminal activities perpetrated.

Our contributions can be summarized as follows:

1. We identify investigation challenges and propose a methodology to choose the most appropriate forensics tools to help drone crime scene investigators.
2. We analyse the acquired drone data using the SOM clustering technique, to help accurately present evidence in the court of law, if there are any unusual activities observed in the flight path.

In our case study, we have implemented SOM for visualising drone data, by reenacting the same procedures of [15] to visually show the data clusters to aid in investigation, and to help predict patterns of criminal behaviour. The maps that are generated in SOM help users to visualize the large volume of high dimensional datasets [18].

2   Background

Drones are vulnerable to various cyber-attacks due to their dependence on the wireless network for communication. In this context, the main challenge faced by many digital forensic investigators is using the appropriate tools for investigating the drone involved in the crime scene. Moreover, there is a lack of study in choosing forensically sound tools based on a given drone model, which plays a vital role in producing valid digital evidence. However, there are reported case studies that focus on the digital investigation process, wherein investigators spend their maximum time in experimenting with various forensic tools to obtain relevant information that can prove the case in the court of law. Hence, there is a need to identify the most appropriate forensic tools for drone forensics, whilst minimizing the incurred investigation process time.

Currently, there are many security vulnerabilities that expose drones to potential malicious attacks by the adversary. UAVs became less expensive in the civilian market for law enforcement, research and entertainment purposes, which caused exposure to novel security threats [6]. Furthermore, in [6], the authors have elaborated upon several cyber incidents and possible countermeasures such as legislative and regulatory initiatives that could be adopted to reduce cyber-attacks against drones.

This case study aims to determine the forensically useful tools to extract efficient artefacts from the DJI Mavic Air drone model. The DJI Mavic Air was developed by DJI (SZ DJI Technology Co., Ltd., China), and has been popularly used in many drone-based consumer markets. This drone model can operate in three different ways, namely, through a dedicated remote controller, from a smartphone, or jointly, which is referred to as GCS (Ground Control Station). DJI Mavic Air is connected to the smartphone via DJI GO 4 for the last two options (DJI, 2020). The main components of Mavic Air are, the aircraft and the GCS; additionally auxiliary components include front LEDs, a MicroSD card slot, a stabilised gimbal, a USB-C port, a 4K resolution camera, four propellers and GPS antennas. The aircraft consists of inbuilt 8 GB internal storage. The DJI Go 4 application provides camera settings adjustment, real-time image transmission and creates flight records in detail for on-device storage. The Mavic Air uses Wireless network for transmission and can fly for 21 min with a maximum flight distance of 10 km [9].

In [5], the author noted that computer forensics as a field of study comprises gathering, retrieving and evaluating of digital data to avoid computer fraud and to preserve digital evidence for further investigation. The author also reported that digital investigation must be conducted in such a manner that enables the information and data collected to be used as evidence for the criminal prosecution of the attacker in the court of law. In [11], the authors state that digital forensics can be classified into three groups namely the source, format and type. The source is nothing but the artefacts that can identify the origin of the information. Maintaining the evidence in its original format is mandatory because there are many tools which can modify it and break the case. Type is one that describes the evidence type such as email, spreadsheet or text message, and format is the data in binary or any other format.

The images acquired from the CFReDS website [21] have been previously used to perform an investigation process in several research papers. In [15], experiments were conducted based on a digital investigation process to include two stages; stage 1 comprises obtaining valid flight path from the gathered evidence from the drone images of CFReDS [21] and stage 2 comprises a clustering technique using the Self-Organising Maps algorithm to augment drone data analysis, where SOM does mapping and placement of similar data items into clusters [17]. In general, the authors have followed five stages of the investigation process, namely, identifying the data/evidence, acquiring/collecting the data identified, preservation of acquired data, examining/analyzing the preserved data and finally, reporting. The results of their studies show that Phantom

4 drones can produce strong evidence compared to Parrot AR Drone 2.0 as it holds valid information to prove a case in the court of law [15]. Similarly, in [8], the authors applied the forensic investigation process comprising, identification, acquisition, preservation, examination and analysis, and presentation of results. They identified that there was a gap between the currently available digital forensics tools and appropriate application of forensics investigation process. Hence the recent findings from [15] are more accurate for producing valid digital evidence and therefore we have followed the same in our case study to analyze the acquired datasets through application of various forensic investigation tools.

3   Proposed Methodology

This section elaborates upon how forensics tools have been widely chosen and methods followed to perform digital forensic analysis of DJI Mavic Air drone data. The methodology followed in this case study is based on [15], according to which, the investigation can be carried out within three steps to obtain information for further analysis. The three steps are acquiring data, drone forensic investigation, acquiring results and reporting.

In our proposed technique, we will be following the same three steps but with a focus on acquiring valid information from the DJI Mavic Air drone datasets using appropriate forensic tools. The Methods followed in our investigation process is as shown in the Fig. 1.

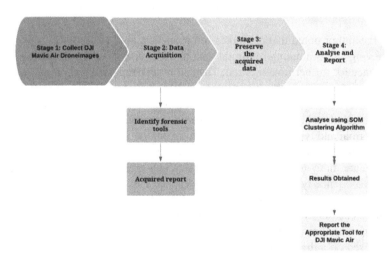

Fig. 1. Drone forensics methodology.

3.1   Collection of DJI Mavic Air Drone Images

The main purpose of this stage is to successfully collect data from the DJI Mavic Air drone images which were obtained from the CFReDS project [21]. All the evidence is stored in the form of forensic images in the data repository, powered by VTO labs [22]. During the first stage, we collected the evidence from the CFReDS repository, i.e., retrieve it. For our study, we have investigated the drone dataset DF048 image of DJI Mavic Air model, comprising two data ranges, 2018_April and 2018_June. These were the most significant datasets for DJI Mavic Air, which is a commonly used drone for both civilian as well as strategic applications. The April 2018 folder has internal memory card information which was physically acquired from the drones, and logical data of android mobile used to operate the DJI Mavic Air drone and backup files associated with the mobile phone operating system. These folders contain evidence which is unaltered and has been verified using the hash code generated through cross validation by both MD5 and SHA1. All data acquired for analysis was live and not synthesized.

3.2 Data Acquisition

Data Acquisition is the process of collating digital evidence as obtained from electronic media. As such, acquisition can be achieved by one of three methods, namely, physically extracting data from devices comprising drones, battery and remote controller; from the flight operator who operates the device, and lastly through sniffing of the communication network between the drone and the backend Cloud storage [15]. In our case study, this is the second stage of the investigation process where valid datasets acquired from DJI Mavic Air, for tool-based analysis.

Forensic tools can be deployed on both structured as well as unstructured data, acquired from raw as well as semi-processed data repositories [15]. As acquisition of heterogeneous data is a cumbersome process, choice of forensic tool plays a crucial role in any investigation process. We have experimented with the following forensic tools to identify the most apt tool to validly analyse the acquired dataset:

Autopsy is an open-source digital investigation tool [27]. The software helps the investigators in providing as much information as possible and helps in segregating the data in the open format according to the given case. It has various features such as case management, image integrity, keyword searching, and other automated operations.

CsvView [25] was released after the release of Datcon with an extra feature of visualizing the .csv file that is produced by converting it into a .DAT file .DatCon is an offline application that can read .DAT file and extract data from the .DAT. The executed output can then be downloaded in Excel, KML and Dashware format for further analysis.

Airdata [24] was previously known as HealthyDrones. It provides the flight operators with an opportunity to analyse their flight path and to help them ensure secured and reliable flights [26]. This application helps the users to automatically upload the flight logs to provide them with immediate visibility to the aircraft's performance and to identify potential underlying issues [26].

3.3 Preserve the Acquired Data

Datasets acquired from the previous step should be preserved in such a way that the evidence should remain unaltered or modified, until the completion of the investigation process. According to [19], there is a well-defined process called the *chain of custody* which states the: when, where, why, who and how, for the evidence collected for the purpose of investigation. Also, this process will ascertain that the evidence is unaltered by any party. Similarly, in [5], it is stated that if an organization decides to prosecute a cybercriminal, additional time and effort needs to be added to the investigation process to make sure that the data and images are adequately preserved. The reason behind the importance of this stage is because it helps in providing admissible evidence in the court of law. Hence the method followed to collect and analyse the evidence is difficult to realise. While the evidence is collected, the investigators must prove its authenticity in its original format, on the criminal's confiscated device, to accurately point out the state of the system at the specified time. Forensic experts must also maintain a proper detailed document of investigation history, comprising collection, managing and preservation of evidence with a log that states the people who encountered this evidence (chain of custody).

Datasets used for our experiments were verified for alterations through hash code analysis using MD5 and SHA1 hash values.

3.4 Analyse and Report

This is the last stage of our investigation process, where analysis of data, raw and processed, is carried out. Machine learning is a common tool for conducting the analysis of captured forensic data. A self-organizing map (SOM) is a type of artificial neural network (ANN) that is trained using unsupervised learning to produce a mapping from one (usually high-dimensional) space to another (usually low-dimensional) space, these trained samples are called a map, and are, therefore useful for reducing data dimensions [20]. In [4], the authors classified the data mining process into six essential steps and described the significance of the SOM for digital forensics. The authors stated that effective visualization and summary of findings is crucial for the investigation, for which self-organizing map would be an excellent tool in the exploratory phase of data mining.

4 Results and Analysis

In this paper, we have experimented with all three data acquisition tools as discussed in Sect. 5. Moreover, we also ran data visualization experiments using SOM, to identify clusters of drone data, to foster investigation.

Files obtained from both drone folders, 2018_April and 2018_June, were initially uploaded into the Autopsy tool by creating a new case with two data sources. However, in the 2018_april folder, there were no flight logs identified, which were required for investigation. Hence, we continued our investigation based on only the 2018_June dataset.

The SD Card-External dataset (DF048.E01) was processed in the ingest module of the tool to extract the following data:

- Deleted files,
- Attached devices to identify the attacker
- Emails associated the device
- Videos and Audios in the SD card
- Images

Once analysis was completed, identified documents were presented, and information was organized through categorization based on type of documents analysed. E.g., e-mail messages and files were categorized based on formats (XML, PDF, .EXE, etc.). Additionally, deleted data was also retrieved, possibly to indict the cybercriminal who may have attempted to conceal his or her traits. An analysis of the Autopsy data yielded data appertaining to deleted files from the SD card, email addresses, video and audio files of the drone device. This data can help investigators to investigate further to identify the attacker by reviewing the email addresses and through further investigation of the deleted files. However, Autopsy does not allow for conversion between .DAT file into .CSV viewable format, which is a disadvantage of this software and investigators need to look for other software which can yield the flight-related information that is derived from .DAT files for their investigation process.

CsvView can accept many log file types such as .txt file, .DAT from many drone products namely Phantom 3, Inspire 1, Mavic Pro, Phantom 4 and Phantom 4 Pro, Inspire 2, Matrice M100, M600, Litchi tablet app, Autologic tablet app and FPV tablet app. This tool is designed to interpret and visualize the uploaded files and has an inbuilt connection to Google Maps API key, which allows the investigators to download imagery from the Google Maps database [16]. Unfortunately, CsvView cannot process onboard .DAT for the Mavic Air, Mavic 2 and Mavic mini drones, which are all found in encrypted formats. In our experiment, we acquired the .DAT file from the mobile device, unencrypted, and hence we decided to use CsvView for the remainder steps of the investigation process.

The .DAT file ("FLY057.DAT"), extracted from the android mobile internal storage, which was used to operate the DJI Mavic Air, was analysed using the "CsvView" tool. After processing through the CSVView tool, which converts the file from a ".DAT" to a ".csv" format, the flights were visualized using the "GeoPlayer" function, which uses the Google Maps API Key as shown in Fig. 2. The GPS data alone is not recorded but also other artefacts were recorded in this drone model, which can be visualized using the CsvView tool [26]. The flight record also had another .DAT file ("FLY058.DAT") which was uploaded to CsvView but we couldn't gain many details from that flight log and hence we proceeded with FLY057.DAT file alone for the remaining experiments.

The flight paths that are extracted by CsvView comprise various attributes that are associated with the direction of the flight path, required for visualizing the flight travel history. Hence, to perform the same, we required some useful information to help us keep track of flight activities. Following are some of the important artefacts obtained from the acquired datasets:

- Offset time
- IMU_ATTI (0): Longitude
- IMU_ATTI (0): Latitude
- IMU_ATTI (0): Voltage
- IMU_ATTI (0): numSats
- GPS (0): Date
- GPS (0): Time
- GPS (0): numGPS
- flyCState
- IMU_ATTI (1): roll

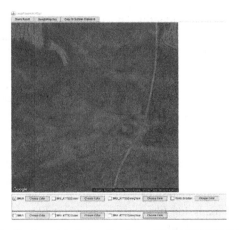

Fig. 2. Annotated visualisation of flight FLY057 [25]

- IMU_ATTI (1): pitch
- IMU_ATTI (1): distance travelled
- IMU_ATTI (1): temperature

The above-mentioned attributes will help investigators to learn about how the flight may have been operated and understand the behaviour of the flight to analyse and apply the SOM clustering algorithm (for visualization of data). The possible artefacts recoverable from these tools are extremely detailed and are more than necessary to analyse a flight record. Those attributes with no significant value associated with them ('0' mostly), were excluded from analysis. The "GeoPlayer" visualization for this flight showed that the GPS data recorded was mostly at par with an actual flight, as shown in Fig. 2. The investigators can analyse further using this tool, by comparing the flight Time series Signals and "numSats" (number of satellites) readings from the flight logs, and during auto takeoff, the "numSats" reading was 0, as shown in the time period (X-Axis) of − 280 to 420 in Fig. 3.

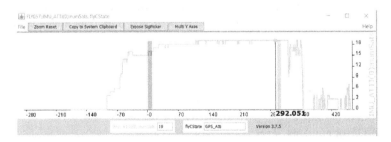

Fig. 3. Data visualization [25]

As a result, we could visualize the flight path and compare it with many other attributes to identify any miscellaneous activities that can be beneficial as piece of valid digital evidence presentable in the court of law. Airdata [24] as such is not popularly used to obtain the valid flight path and attributes associated with drone images. The datasets retrieved from the flight paths of DJI Mavic Air are larger in size and carry more useful information to support the investigation. In our case study, we uploaded the .DAT file (FLY057.DAT) to obtain the flight paths and its related datasets.

As a result, we could obtain the final report in .CSV format to yield valid datasets for further investigation based upon the attributes; power, battery level, and drone model with version, maximum distance, altitude and total kilometers covered during this flight path, as shown in Fig. 4.

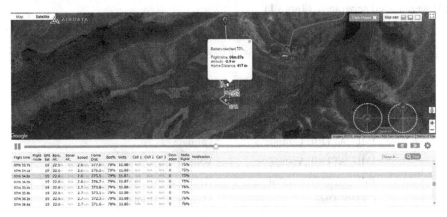

Fig. 4. Flight path with battery level information [24].

Digital investigators can easily obtain the datasets associated with the flight record by using this tool as it produces all the useful information which can be downloaded in many formats such as KML, GPX, CSV as well as the original format. The battery usage is recorded all through the flight period. The attributes that are extracted from the datasets are associated with the direction of the flight path is required for visualizing the flight travel history. Hence, to perform the same, we required some useful information that helps us to track the flight log. Following are some of the important artefacts acquired from these datasets:

- DateTime
- Longitude
- Latitude
- Voltage
- Height_above_takeoff (feet)
- Maximum Altitude
- Maximum speed
- Maximum distance
- flyCstate
- Roll (degrees)
- Pitch (degrees)

- Distance (feet)
- Battery Temperature

Now we present the results obtained from the flight path information of the DJI Mavic Air (FLY057) acquired from CsvView and Airdata [24] tools by selecting some important attributes of the datasets that are then injected for training into the SOM implementation on the Weka platform [23], which is popularly used for data mining research [14].

Insignificant data attributes for the drone data were removed in Weka [23], followed by training and clustering using SOM. Attributes obtained from CsvView and AirData [24] were tested separately (Table 1).

Table 1. Reduced attribute list

CsvView attributes	AirData attributes
offsetTime	Date Time
IMU_ATTI(0):Longitude	Longitude
IMU_ATTI(0):Latitude	Latitude
IMU_ATTI(0):Voltage	Voltage
IMU_ATTI(0):numSats	Height_above_takeoff(feet)
GPS(0):Date	Maximum Altitude
GPS(0):Time	Maximum speed
GPS(0):numGPS	Maximum distance
flyCState	flyCstate
IMU_ATTI(1):roll	Roll (degrees)
IMU_ATTI(1):pitch	Pitch (degrees)
IMU_ATTI(1):distanceTravelled	Distance (feet)
IMU_ATTI(1):temperature	Battery temperature

Plots that are illustrated in Figs. 5, and 6, are generated based on the results obtained when the valid flight dataset (FLY057) obtained from the two forensic tools (CSVView and AirData), are presented as input to the SOM clustering algorithm. The x-axis represents the instance number of the GPS coordinates of the flight path, and the y-axis represents the corresponding latitudes.

Based on analysis of the above plots, we observe a minor difference in both the drone flight paths for the two acquisition tools tested, and many artefacts were found to be similar in both CsvView based plots as well as the Airdata [24] based plots, such as the flight paths obtained through GPS coordinates. But, in terms of accuracy in gaining the flight details, Airdata.com was found to be more accurate for DJI drones, which we could compare from [15], where the authors had conducted similar experiments on the Phantom 4 drone images. In their experiment, they identified that DJI Phantom 4 to

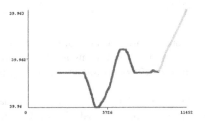
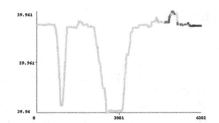

Fig. 5. CsvView-FLY057 plot [23]   **Fig. 6.** Airdata -FLY057 plot [23]

have valid flight paths which were compared with the Ardupilot DIY drone model. As per their obtained results, they had extracted the flight paths using Airdata.com for DJI Phantom 4 which yielded a good dataset visualization in their final experimental results.

DJI Mavic Air has advanced sensors and a high-resolution camera, through which data can be recorded in many different modes while operating the flight, namely, Motors Started, Auto Takeoff, Go Home, Auto Landing and Confirm Landing. However, each dataset in CsvView comprised only a few data points, for DJI Mavic Air, when compared to the data obtained for Airdata, which could also be another reason that data obtained from airdata.com was found to be more informative. For Airdata, the SOM clusters were found to be formed in a way that the datasets are organised perfectly, which holds initial stages of the flight path and also holds the maximum distance, speed, altitude and ascent, including high battery temperature to depict the final stages of the flight journey. Based on the results obtained from both the tools by applying the SOM clustering algorithm on the respective datasets, results obtained from the Airdata tool [24] have yielded higher accuracy and would help investigators to better predict the flight paths based on clustered data points as inputs. Information obtained from Autopsy can be useful in such scenarios to indict the cybercriminal, with solid evidence provided to support the criminal charges against the suspect.

5   Conclusions and Future Work

The digital forensics investigation process is heavily reliant on tools. A significant issue remains on choice of the most apt forensic tool, to help invetigators carry out their tasks. Even though, many studies have shown various investigation processes adopted, using a clustering algorithm such as Self-Organising Maps has been previously tested to analyse the drone data successfully acquired. In this paper, we addressed the problem of identifying essential forensic tools for drones, with particular experiment carried out on DJI Mavic Air drone data. As a part of the investigation process, extracted datasets from three different forensic tools namely, Airdata, Autopsy and CsvView for DJI Mavic Air were presented as input to the SOM clustering algorithm. Results obtained identify Airdata.com and Autopsy tools as stronger candidates for analysis of relevant drone artefacts when compared to the CsvView tool, due to their ability to foster unsupervised data classification on the acquired drone data, by yielding strong insights into the acquired drone dataset when compared to CsvView. As part of our future work, we intend to identify forensically sound tools for forensic investigation of other cutting-edge drone models.

References

1. Iqbal, F., Alam, S., Kazim, A., MacDermott, Á.: Drone forensics: a case study on DJI phantom 4. In: IEEE/ACS 16th International Conference on Computer Systems and Applications (AICCSA), Abu Dhabi, United Arab Emirates, pp. 1–6 (2019). https://doi.org/10.1109/aiccsa47632.2019.9035302
2. Vattapparamban, E., Güvenç, İ., Yurekli, A.İ., Akkaya, K., Uluağaç, S.: Drones for smart cities: issues in cybersecurity, privacy, and public safety. In: International Wireless Communications and Mobile Computing Conference (IWCMC), Paphos, pp. 216–221 (2016), https://doi.org/10.1109/iwcmc.2016.7577060
3. Bouafif, H., Kamoun, F., Iqbal, F., Marrington, A.: Drone forensics: challenges and new insights. In: 9th IFIP International Conference on New Technologies, Mobility and Security (NTMS), pp. 1–6 (2018). https://doi.org/10.1109/ntms.2018.8328747
4. Vesanto, J., Alhoniemi, E.: Clustering of the self-organizing map. IEEE Trans. Neural Netw. **11**(3), 586–600 (2000). https://doi.org/10.1109/72.846731
5. Ali, K.M.: Digital forensics best practices and managerial implications. In: 4th International Conference on Computational Intelligence, Communication Systems and Networks, CICSyN, pp. 196–199. https://doi.org/10.1109/cicsyn.2012.44
6. Hartmann, K., Giles, K.: UAV exploitation: a new domain for cyber power. In: Pissanidis, N., Rõigas, H., Veenendaal, M. (eds.), 8th International Conference on Cyber Conflict: Cyber Power, pp. 205–221 (2016). https://doi.org/10.1109/cycon.2016.7529436
7. Azhar, M.A.H.B., Hannan, A., Barton, T., Islam, T.: Drone forensic analysis using open source tools. J. Digit. Forensics Secur. Law **13**(1), 6 (2018). https://doi.org/10.15394/jdfsl.2018.1513
8. Harbawi, M., Varol, A.: The role of digital forensics in combating cybercrimes. In: Proceedings of the 4th International Symposium on Digital Forensics and Security Little Rock, AR, pp. 138–142 (2016). https://doi.org/10.1109/isdfs.2016.7473532
9. Yousef, M., Iqbal, F.: Drone forensics: a case study on a DJI Mavic Air. In: IEEE/ACS 16th International Conference on Computer Systems and Applications (AICCSA), Abu Dhabi, United Arab Emirates, pp. 1–3 (2019), https://doi.org/10.1109/aiccsa47632.2019.9035365
10. Wazid, M., Katal, A., Goudar, R.H., Rao, S.: Hacktivism trends, digital forensic tools and challenges: a survey. In: 2013 IEEE Conference on Information & Communication Technologies, Thuckalay, Tamil Nadu, India, pp. 138–144 (2013), https://doi.org/10.1109/cict.2013.6558078
11. Reeva, P., Siddhesh, D., Preet, G., Pratik, S., Jain, N.: Digital forensics capability analyzer: a tool to check forensic capability: In: International Conference on Nascent Technologies in Engineering (ICNTE), Navi Mumbai, India, pp. 1–7 (2019). https://doi.org/10.1109/icnte44896.2019.8945960
12. Finn, R.L., Wright, D.: Privacy, data protection and ethics for civil drone practice: a survey of industry, regulators and civil society organisations. Comput. Law Secur. Rev. **32**, 577–586 (2016). https://doi.org/10.1016/j.clsr.2016.05.010
13. Hall, M., Frank, E., Holmes, G., Pfahringer, B., Reutemann, P., Witten, I.H.: The weka data mining software: an update. SIGKDD Explor. News **11**, 10–18 (2009). https://doi.org/10.1145/1656274.1656278
14. Singal, S., Jena, M.: A study on WEKA tool for data pre-processing, classification and clustering. Int. J. Innovative Tech. Explor. Eng. (IJITEE) **2**(6), 250–253 (2013)
15. Mekala, S.H., Baig, Z.: Digital forensics for drone data – intelligent clustering using self organising maps. In: Doss, R., Piramuthu, S., Zhou, W. (eds.) FNSS 2019. CCIS, vol. 1113, pp. 172–189. Springer, Cham (2019). https://doi.org/10.1007/978-3-030-34353-8_13

16. Barton, T.E.A., Azhar, M.A.H.B.: Open Source Forensics for a Multi-platform Drone System. In: Matoušek, P., Schmiedecker, M. (eds.) ICDF2C 2017. LNICSSITE, vol. 216, pp. 83–96. Springer, Cham (2018). https://doi.org/10.1007/978-3-319-73697-6_6
17. Zhangi, X.-Y., Chen, J.-S., Dong, J.-K.: Color clustering using self-organizing maps. In: Proceedings of the 2007 International Conference on Wavelet Analysis and Pattern Recognition, Beijing, China, vol. 3, pp. 986–989 (2007). https://doi.org/10.1109/icwapr.2007.4421574
18. Feyereisl, J., Aickelin, U.: Self-organizing maps in computer security, arXiv.org, arXiv:1608.01668 (2016)
19. Rana, N., Sansanwal, G., Khatter, K., Singh, S.: Taxonomy of digital forensics: investigation tools and challenges. eprint arXiv:1709.06529 (2017)
20. Berglund, E., Sitte, J.: The parameterless self-organizing map algorithm. IEEE Trans. Neural Netw. **17**(2), 305–316 (2006). https://doi.org/10.1109/TNN.2006.871720
21. U.S. Commerce Department, The CFReDS Project, NIST (2019). Accessed 20 Mar 2020. https://www.cfreds.nist.gov
22. United States Department of Homeland Security (DHS) Science and Technology Directorate, Cyber Security Division (DHS S&T/CSD) 2018, The Drone Forensic Program, VTO Inc. Accessed 20 Mar 2020. https://www.vtolabs.com
23. University of Waikato, Weka (1993). Accessed 2 May 2020. https://www.cs.waikato.ac.nz/ml/weka/
24. Steiner, E.: Airdata UAV (2015). Accessed 15 Apr 2020. https://airdata.com/
25. Csv 2017, Csv View Downloads. Accessed 15 Apr 2020. https://datfile.net/
26. Gaylord, B.: HealthyDrones is now Airdata UAV (2017). Accessed 20 May 2020. https://airdata.com/blog/2017/healthydrones-is-now-airdata-uav
27. Carrier, B.: Open source digital forensics tools-the legal argument (2002). Accessed 20 Apr 2020. www.atstake.com/research/reports/acrobat/atstake_opensource_forensics.pdf
28. Carrier, B.: Autospy, Basis Technology (2003). Accessed 15 Apr 2020. https://www.sleuthkit.org/autopsy/
29. Cavoukian, A.: Privacy and drones: unmanned aerial vehicles. Information and Privacy Commissioner of Ontario, Canada Ontario (2007). Accessed 20 May 2020. https://www.ipc.on.ca/

Distinguishing Attacks on Linearly Filtered NFSRs with Decimated Output

Matthew Beighton$^{(\boxtimes)}$ ⓘ, Harry Bartlett ⓘ, Leonie Simpson ⓘ,
and Kenneth Koon-Ho Wong ⓘ

Queensland University of Technology, Brisbane, QLD, Australia
matthew.beighton@hdr.qut.edu.au

Abstract. This paper presents an investigation into the resistance of linearly filtered nonlinear feedback shift registers (LF-NFSRs) against distinguishing attacks. We formalise the method described by Orumiehchiha, Pieprzyk, Steinfeld and Bartlett and then extend it to develop a more efficient, systematic framework for accurately distinguishing an arbitrary LF-NFSR. Our method is then generalised to distinguish arbitrary LF-NFSRs with regularly decimated output sequences. The proposed method is demonstrated through application to the example LF-NFSR used by Orumiehchiha et al. with improved results. Additionally, our new method can be accurately applied to much larger registers and can predict how much output is needed to find the strongest bias. To demonstrate this, we derive time and keystream requirement estimates for our attacks on each variant of the Grain family of stream ciphers under weak key-IV pairs.

Keywords: Nonlinear feedback shift register · Linearly filtered NFSR · Distinguishing attack · Decimated sequences · Grain

1 Introduction

Lightweight cryptographic algorithms have gained significant attention in recent times due to their potential for application in small and fast hardware. Stream ciphers are symmetric key algorithms capable of providing high speed bit-wise encryption to sensitive data with minimal hardware and run time costs. Traditional stream cipher designs used register based keystream generators.

One traditional stream cipher design is the nonlinear filter generator (NLFG), which uses a single linear feedback shift register (LFSR) together with a nonlinear filter function. Keystream is generated by applying the nonlinear function to the state of the LFSR.

More recent cipher designs incorporate nonlinear state update to mitigate certain attacks, including algebraic attacks that exploited the linearity of LFSRs. The dual construction of the NLFG consists of a nonlinear feedback shift register (NFSR) with a linear filter function. These constructions are known as linearly filtered nonlinear feedback shift registers (LF-NFSRs).

© Springer Nature Singapore Pte Ltd. 2020
L. Batina and G. Li (Eds.): ATIS 2020, CCIS 1338, pp. 42–60, 2020.
https://doi.org/10.1007/978-981-33-4706-9_4

Berbain, Gilbert and Joux [4] have shown that LF-NFSRs are also susceptible to both algebraic and correlation attacks, with both attack methods resulting in key recovery. A distinguishing attack on LF-NFSRs has also been presented [32]. The well known Grain family of stream ciphers uses a NFSR as a component in the keystream generator and behaves as a LF-NFSR under certain circumstances. Trivium [9] operates as a linear filtered system of NFSRs, while other ciphers, such as Plantlet [30], Fruit [2] and Sprout [3] have similar structures to Grain. The most recent variants of Grain (Grain-128a and Grain-128AEAD) use every second bit of keystream for authentication purposes. Traditional distinguishing attack methods no longer apply to this decimation of the keystream sequence. In this paper, we provide a general systematic method for distinguishing the output of an arbitrary LF-NFSR from a random binary sequence. We then generalise the traditional distinguishing methods to allow for distinguishing attacks on LF-NFSRs with decimated output sequences. Our attack is then applied to every variant of Grain when initialised using a weak key-IV pair.

This paper is organised as follows: Sect. 2 provides an overview of shift registers and introduces the notation used in this paper. Section 3 describes filter generators and sequence decimation. Section 4 describes the use of linear functions to approximate nonlinear functions. We present our method for distinguishing a LF-NFSR in Sect. 5 (for both consecutive and regularly decimated output sequences), followed by a worked example in Sect. 6. The new generalised distinguishing attack is applied to the Grain family under special conditions in Sect. 7. Finally, we conclude the paper in Sect. 8.

2   Feedback Shift Registers

2.1   Stages and State

A feedback shift register (FSR) of length n is a set of n storage devices called *stages* $(r_0, r_1, ..., r_{n-1})$ together with a Boolean update function g. For binary shift registers, each stage of the register holds a value from the set $\{0,1\}$. We denote the initial state of the register S^0, which consists of initial state bits $s_0, s_1, ..., s_{n-1}$. The state at any time t is defined to be S^t. The sequence of state bits that passes through the register R over time is denoted S; that is $S = s_0, s_1, ..., s_{n-1}, s_n, ...$. All bits s_{n+t}, $t \geq 0$ are referred to as update bits.

2.2   State Update

The register state is updated by introducing a "shift" using a clocking system. The registers investigated in this paper are regularly clocked fibonacci style, as shown in Fig. 1. At each clock, the content of stage r_i is shifted to stage r_{i-1} for $1 \leq i \leq n-1$ and the contents of stage r_0 is lost from the register. The new content of stage r_{n-1} (referred to as the register feedback) must be inserted. The Boolean feedback $g(r_0, r_1, .., r_{n-1})$ is applied to the current state to compute the bit value to be inserted in r_{n-1}. If g is linear, then the register is said to be a linear feedback shift register (LFSR) and if g is nonlinear, then the register is said to be a nonlinear feedback shift register (NFSR).

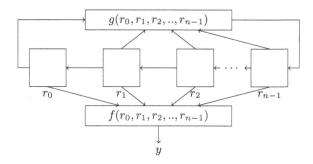

Fig. 1. A n-stage feedback shift register with Boolean update function g and filter function f.

2.3 Output

A binary sequence can be generated from a FSR by outputting a single bit from the register at each time step. As shown in Fig. 1, each output bit y_t is generated by applying a Boolean function f to the state S^t. A simple way to produce output from a FSR is to choose $f = r_0$ which is shifted out of the register at each time step. Alternatively, the output can be a function of multiple register stages.

3 Filter Generators and Sequences

Registers where f is a function of the contents of multiple stages in R results in a design called a *filter generator*. Traditionally, keystream generators for stream ciphers used a LFSR together with a filter function f. It is easy to show that if the filter function for a LFSR is chosen to be linear, the filter generator provides no more security than a single LFSR. LFSRs, when used by themselves as keystream generators, provide very little security to the plaintext [28]. For this reason, LFSRs were traditionally filtered using a nonlinear Boolean function.

3.1 Nonlinear Filter Generators

A LFSR filtered by a nonlinear function f, is known as a *nonlinear filter generator* (NLFG) [35]. The security of nonlinear filter generators has been extensively analysed in the public literature. These designs have been shown to be susceptible to a number of attacks including: correlation attacks [16,18,29,35], algebraic attacks [7,8,14] and distinguishing attacks [13]. The successful attacks show that the properties of the nonlinear filter function directly determine the resistance of the NLFG against cryptanalysis. The underlying LFSR provides only the desirable statistical properties. Given that a single Boolean function cannot display high levels of all desirable cryptographic properties, choosing a filter function that resists one attack may leave it vulnerable to other attacks [31].

In response to the successful cryptanalysis of NLFGs, designs using NFSRs were proposed. While nonlinear state update functions can mitigate the vulnerability exploited, the overall structure of sequences produced by NFSRs are not completely understood.

3.2 Linearly Filtered Nonlinear Feedback Shift Registers

A more recent proposal is the dual construction of the nonlinear filter generator; where the update function g to the register is nonlinear and the filter function f is linear [17]. This design is known as a linearly filtered nonlinear feedback shift register (LF-NFSR). In this paper, where the filter function f is a linear function, we use L to denote the function. Given that LF-NFSRs use only one nonlinear function, it is interesting to investigate the role of the nonlinear function in providing higher levels of security to the output sequence. In this paper we examine the security of LF-NFSRs with respect to distinguishing attacks.

3.3 Decimated Sequences

Another traditional way of providing nonlinear keystream sequences using LFSRs is through sequence decimation. An example of this is the shrinking generator [6]. The shrinking generator consists of two regularly clocked LFSRs; register one is used to select which bits are used as output (keystream) from register two. If the output of register one is a 1, then the output of register two is used, otherwise it is discarded. Ultimately, the output sequence consists of a "shrunk-down" version of the sequence produced by register two [24]. The sequence produced by the shrinking generator can be considered as a irregularly decimated version of the output sequence of register two.

In this paper LF-NFSRs with regularly decimated output sequences will be of interest. To investigate the output of these devices successfully we need to be able to refer to the full output sequence and the decimated output sequence. For this we denote the full output sequence of the LF-NFSR as $y = \{y_i\}_{i=0}^{\infty}$ and the decimated output sequence as $z = \{z_k\}_{k=0}^{\infty}$. Without loss of generality, in this paper we assume $z_0 = y_0$. That is, we assume the first bit of the decimated sequence is the first bit of the full output sequence. We say that $\{z_k\}_{k=0}^{\infty}$ is a ψ-decimated sequence of $\{y_i\}_{i=0}^{\infty}$ if $\{z_i\}_{i=0}^{\infty} = \{y_{\psi i}\}_{i=0}^{\infty}$.

4 Nonlinear Functions, Linear Approximations and Bias

If a given nonlinear function can be accurately approximated by a linear function, then the cryptanalysis that applies in the linear case can be applied with some probability in the nonlinear case. The Walsh-Hadamard Transformation (WHT) is useful here as it expresses a Boolean function uniquely in terms of its correlation with all linear functions [34]. The WHT will return a set of values, where each entry corresponds to a unique linear function. Any nonzero value appearing for a given entry represents a bias ϵ.

For a bias ϵ, the probability that the linear function is equal to the nonlinear function (over the set of all possible input values) is given by $\frac{1}{2} + \epsilon$. The entry with the highest absolute bias is considered the best linear approximation. For further discussion on the WHT the interested reader is referred elsewhere [11,15,34].

5   General Distinguishing Attack

If a binary sequence is truly random, the probability that any given bit will be a 0 or a 1 is 0.5. Furthermore, the probability that any combination of bits will be a 0 or a 1 is also 0.5. The binary sequence produced by a keystream generator of a stream cipher is intended to mimic the One Time Pad [24]. That is, the sequence should be indistinguishable from random. A distinguishing attack aims to determine whether a given segment of a binary sequence was generated randomly, or by a specific deterministic algorithm. If no distinction can be made as to which source produced the output, the algorithm in question is theoretically secure against distinguishing attacks [33].

Given that every stream cipher uses a finite key, there will always exist a distinguishing attack provided enough keystream is available. A distinguishing attack can be broken into two phases: pre-computation and online. For the pre-computation phase, an attacker needs to understand the structure of the cipher being attacked. In particular, they need to know the Boolean functions that the cipher uses and how it uses them. In the online phase, the attacker needs to observe a segment of keystream. The length of keystream required for a successful distinguishing attack depends on the Boolean functions used to build the cipher. Ciphers designed with cryptographically weak Boolean functions that are vulnerable to distinguishing attacks, may leak information that leads to stronger successful attacks.

In this paper we consider that the LF-NFSR may be a component of a keystream generator for a stream cipher. We investigate potential distinguishing attacks on such a LF-NFSR. We will consider the case where consecutive bits of output are observed by an attacker, as well as the case where a regularly decimated output sequence is observed. Furthermore, we assume that the internal state of the register is not observed, either initially or during output generation.

Orumiehchiha, Pieprzyk, Steinfeld and Bartlett described a method for distinguishing a LF-NFSR with consecutive observable output bits [32] through an example. We refer to this method as the OPSB method. In this paper we first formalise the OPSB method and then provide a more efficient method for finding a strong bias in the output sequence.

5.1   OPSB Method

In [32], the OPSB method is presented through application to an example LF-NFSR, constructed using a NFSR of length $n = 7$ and a linear filter function that takes input from four of the seven stages of the NFSR. The OPSB method builds two systems of equations; one using L (previously described by Berbain et al.) and another using the best linear approximation for g. Subsets of the two systems are combined to generate a new system of equations, with each equation a linear combination of initial state bits and output bits that is equal to zero. Note that each equation in the system built using the best linear approximation will be probabilistic and so, the final system will also be probabilistic.

5.2   Generalised Method

The OPSB method seems to use an ad hoc approach to determining which equations from the final system to add together. In the following section we provide an efficient, systematic way of selecting the equations. We now present our generalised method for distinguishing a LF-NFSR.

Identifying a bias in the output bits is achieved in the following way:

Step 1. A system of equations is developed using L to represent every update bit as a linear combination of a subset of the initial state bits and some output bits.

Step 2. A system of equations is developed using the best linear approximation for g to represent each update bit in terms of a subset of the initial state bits and output bits. The equations in this system will be probabilistic, with probabilities based on the bias associated with the linear approximation.

Step 3. Subsets of the two systems are added to one another to generate a new system. This final system consists of a set of linear combinations of initial state bits and output bits, equal to zero.

Step 4. From this new system, a matrix of coefficients in the initial state bits is created.

Step 5. A basis for the row space of this matrix is identified (that is, all equations that are linear combinations of others in terms of the initial state bits are identified).

Step 6. The linearly dependent rows of this matrix correspond to sums of equations that correspond to biased equation in the output bits only. The lower the weight of the sum, the stronger the bias will be.

Note that steps 1–3 effectively describe the OPSB method. In steps 4–6, we provide a systematic approach to identify the strongest bias. We now discuss each step in detail.

Step 1: Develop a System of Equations Using L

Developing a system of equations using L was first described by Berbain et al. [4].

Input: $S^0 = s_0, ..., s_{n-1}, \{y_t\}_{t=0}^{\infty}$

Process:

1. Consider y_0, the output at time $t = 0$, produced by the application of the linear filter function to the register contents.

$$y_0 = L(s_0, ..., s_{n-1}) = \sum_{k=0}^{n-1} a_k s_k$$

where a_k are coefficients from the set $\{0,1\}$.

There will exist a highest indexed term in this sum, s_j, such that $a_j = 1$. Denote the index of this term by j. Now consider the first output bit y_0. We have the following:

$$y_0 = s_j + \sum_{k=0}^{j-1} a_k s_k$$

2. We can rearrange this equation to represent s_j as a sum of an output bit and initial state bits.

$$s_j = \sum_{k=0}^{j-1} a_k s_k + y_0$$

3. Repeating this process for all subsequent time steps, allows us to express every bit s_{j+t}, $t \geq 0$ in terms of output bits and initial state bits. We now have a set of equations of the form:

$$s_{j+t} = \sum_{k=0}^{j-1} a_{k+t} s_{k+t} + y_t,$$

for $t \geq 0$. Note that if later summations contain any bit for which an equation already exists, we can replace this bit with the corresponding linear combination of initial state bits. We denote the system developed using function L as system $\mathcal{L}$.

Output: system $\mathcal{L}$

Step 2: Develop a System Using a Linear Approximation for g

Input: $S^0 = s_0, ..., s_{n-1}$, $\{y_t\}_{t=0}^{\infty}$, system $\mathcal{L}$

Process:

1. Identify the best linear approximation for g, namely $\widetilde{g}$ (with bias ϵ). Note that there may exist more than one linear approximation for g with bias ϵ. The case where there exist multiple best linear approximations is discussed in Sect. 5.5.
2. Using the linear approximation $\widetilde{g}$ with bias ϵ, we can represent s_{n+t}, $t \geq 0$ by

$$s_{n+t} = \widetilde{g}(s_{0+t}, \ldots, s_{n-1+t})$$

with some probability $P = \frac{1}{2} + \epsilon$. Note that if the equation for s_{n+t} contains variables s_i with index j or higher, we can replace them using the corresponding equation in system $\mathcal{L}$, to give an equation that contains only the initial state bits. We denote the resulting system from this process as system $\widetilde{\mathcal{G}}$.

Output: system $\widetilde{\mathcal{G}}$

On completing Step 2, we have two systems of equations (system $\mathcal{L}$ and the newly created system $\widetilde{\mathcal{G}}$) that relate update bits to initial state bits and output bits. Note that the system developed using $\widetilde{g}$ will have $n - j$ fewer equations than that developed using L.

Step 3: Create a System of the Sum of System L and System $\widetilde{\mathcal{G}}$

Input: system $\mathcal{L}$, system $\widetilde{\mathcal{G}}$

Process:

1. Produce a new system of equations by adding a subset of system $\mathcal{L}$ to system $\widetilde{\mathcal{G}}$. Each equation in both $\mathcal{L}$ and system $\widetilde{\mathcal{G}}$ represents a state bit in the sequence S. The systems are combined by matching up equations that correspond to the same state bit and adding them together. We denote the final system as system $\mathcal{L} + \widetilde{\mathcal{G}}$, which will now be a system equal to 0.

Output: system $\mathcal{L} + \widetilde{\mathcal{G}}$

Step 4: Create the Coefficient Matrix
The new system (system $\mathcal{L} + \widetilde{\mathcal{G}}$) contains unknown initial state bits and known output bits. Our objective in Step 4 is to identify a linear combination of the equations in system $\widetilde{\mathcal{G}}$ that annihilates the initial state bits, leaving a sum of output bits that is equal to zero.

Input: system $\mathcal{L} + \widetilde{\mathcal{G}}$

Process:

1. Create a matrix M, where the entries in each row correspond to the coefficients of the initial state bits in the corresponding equation. The number of columns in M is therefore equal to j (as any initial state bit with index higher than j can be represented in terms of initial state bits with lower indices and output bits). The number of rows in M is equal to the number of equations in system $\mathcal{L} + \widetilde{\mathcal{G}}$ and is governed by the number of output bits available to the attacker.

Output: M

Step 5: Identify a Linear Dependency

Input: M

Process:

1. Transpose M and generate the reduced row echelon form. This will reveal (in terms of the initial state bits):
   - A basis for the row space of M
   - The linearly dependent rows of M
   - Which linear combination of the basis rows produces each of these
   We will refer to the reduced row echelon form of M^T as M'.

Output: M'

Step 6: Determine a Bias

Input: M'

Process:

1. Identifying a linear dependent row corresponds to finding a sum of equations such that all initial state bits cancel. Adding these equations together results in an equation consisting of a linear combination of output bits that is equal to zero.

Output: Linear combination of output bits equal to zero.

5.3   Distinguishing a LF-NFSR with Regularly Decimated Output

The distinguishing attack on the output sequence of a LF-NFSR described in Sect. 5.2 can be modified to distinguish a segment of regularly decimated LF-NFSR output from a randomly generated sequence. Simply, we will now have more unknowns in system $\mathcal{L} + \widetilde{\mathcal{G}}$ corresponding to the output bits that aren't observed.

To begin, system $\mathcal{L} + \widetilde{\mathcal{G}}$ is built exactly as described in Sect. 5.2. The structure of system $\mathcal{L} + \widetilde{\mathcal{G}}$ depends only on the Boolean functions used in the LF-NFSR. It does not depend on whether or not the original output sequence is decimated, nor does it depend on how the sequence is decimated. The final system will contain variables for every bit in $\{y_i\}_{i=0}^{\infty}$. What the decimation will change though, is the output y_i that are observable by the attacker. That is, the set of variables that can be substituted for in the online phase of the attack. Thus, for a distinguishing attack on a LF-NFSR with a regularly decimated output sequence, the indices of the observable output bits (with respect to the sequence $\{y_i\}_{i=0}^{\infty}$) must be known to the attacker.

When a regularly decimated output sequence is observed, the system created using the method described in Sect. 5.2 will contain: unknown initial state bits, unknown output bits and observed output bits. We are interested in finding a linear combination of the equations in system $\mathcal{L} + \widetilde{\mathcal{G}}$ that annihilates the initial state bits and the unknown output bits, leaving a sum of observed output bits that is equal to zero.

To find a linear combination which results in a bias in the observed output bits, a matrix M is created whose entries in each row correspond to the coefficients of the initial state bits and unknown output bits in the corresponding equation. The number of rows in the matrix M therefore depends on the number of output bits available to the attacker.

Determining the Dimension of M. To begin, suppose that the output sequence is regularly decimated using a decimation of length ψ. That is, $\{z_i\}_{i=0}^{\infty} = \{y_{\psi i}\}_{i=0}^{\infty}$.

Lemma 1. For a ψ-decimated sequence, the number of columns in M is given by $j + (q - 1)(\psi - 1)$ and the number of rows is given by $\psi(q - 1) + 1$, where q denotes the number of observed output bits and j is the index of the highest indexed term in L.

Proof. For a ψ-decimated sequence, every equation will introduce a new variable into the system (corresponding to an unknown output bit) except if the index of the highest indexed output bit is congruent to 0 mod ψ. That is, $\psi - 1$ new unknown output bits will appear in between each observed output bit. The number of columns in M when an ψ-decimated sequence is observed is therefore given by $j + (q - 1)(\psi - 1)$. The number of rows in M is equal to the number of equations in the new system and is given by $\psi(q - 1) + 1$.

Provided the number of rows in M exceeds the number of columns, Step 5 of Sect. 5.2 will be successful. It therefore follows that if more than j bits of output are observed, a bias can always be identified in the output. This is true regardless of the size of ψ, or if the sequence is regularly decimated. That is, even if the sequence is irregularly decimated in some way, at most $j + 1$ bits of output (for which the indices with respect to $\{y_i\}_{i=0}^{\infty}$ are known) must be observed to guarantee that a bias equation can be identified.

Identifying a Bias. Biased equations are identified using a process analogous to Step 5, when consecutive output bits are observed. However, for regularly decimation, the matrix M contains entries for both the initial state bits and the unknown output bits. Identifying a linearly dependent row of M corresponds to finding a sum of equations equal to zero, with regard to the initial state bits and unknown output bits. Adding these equations together will leave some combination of observed output bits equal to zero. As in Sect. 5.2, we will refer to the reduced row echelon form of M^T as M'.

5.4   Choosing the Best Linear Combination

Regardless of the type of is decimation, each equation in system $\mathcal{L} + \widetilde{\mathcal{G}}$ produced by using the linear approximation $\widetilde{g}$. Thus, each equation is probabilistic with probability $\frac{1}{2} + \epsilon$ of being true. We denote the event that the equation is true as E. The probability of E is determined by the number of equations in that linear combination and can be calculated using the piling up lemma. The piling up lemma states that the probability of a sum of probabilistic equations being correct is given by:

$$p = \Pr(E) = \frac{1}{2} + 2^{e-1}(\epsilon)^e$$

where e is the number of equations used in the linear combination and ϵ is the bias of each equation. Thus, the bias of the combined equation is $b = 2^{e-1}(\epsilon)^e$.

As discussed by Hell, Johansson and Brynielsson [19], when b is small, the number of keystream bits required to distinguish the LF-NFSR is approximately equal to $\frac{1}{b^2}$. Clearly the distinguishing attack is most successful when e is minimised.

A Note on Systems Without Decimation: As highlighted in step 1 of Sect. 5.2, the linear filter function L will have a highest indexed term. Recall that the index of this term is denoted j. Using this, we were able generate the following equation that holds for every $t \geq 0$:

$$s_{j+t} = \sum_{k=0}^{j-1} a_{k+t} s_{k+t} + y_t.$$

Obviously, there can be at most j independent state variables $(s_0, ..., s_{j-1})$ in this equation. Thus, there are at most 2^j combinations of these variables. It clearly follows that in the system developed using L, namely *system $\mathcal{L}$*, there can be at most 2^j steps before a combination of state variables is repeated. In fact, because the all zero combination would correspond simply to bits of output and given that the system will always start with a nonzero combination, there can be at most $2^j - 1$ steps before a combination of state variables is repeated. The maximum period of $2^j - 1$ for a chosen index j can only be achieved in *system $\mathcal{L}$* if the linear filter function L is primitive over $\mathbb{F}_{2^j}$. Note that even though a NFSR of length n is capable of producing a sequence of length 2^n, the use of the linear filter function L means that *system $\mathcal{L}$* acts like a register of length j. Given that the maximum value for j is $n - 1$, the maximum period overall for *system $\mathcal{L}$* is $2^{n-1} - 1$.

We note also that because *system $\mathcal{G}$* substitutes update bits using equations from *system $\mathcal{L}$*, *system $\mathcal{G}$* and *system $\mathcal{L} + \mathcal{G}$* will share the same period as *system $\mathcal{L}$*. Thus, *system $\mathcal{L} + \mathcal{G}$* will be periodic in the state variables, with period less than or equal to $2^j - 1$.

If an attacker has access to 2^j bits of output, the final system is guaranteed to have repeated itself in terms of the initial state bits. It follows that if an attacker has access to 2^j bits of output they are guaranteed to find the lowest weight linear combination that produces a bias in the output, namely, a linear combination of two equations, with a combined bias $b = 2\epsilon^2$. This observation does not hold for decimated sequences as new output variables are introduced into the system over time.

General Process: To minimise e, we look back at the columns of M'. Note that there will be $j + (q - 1)(\psi - 1)$ basis elements, because every state variable beyond s_j can be represented as a linear combination from the set $\{s_0, s_1..., s_j\}$ and the set of output bits. Thus, the first $j + (q - 1)(\psi - 1)$ columns of M' will correspond to the basis elements of the row space of M, in terms of the initial state variables. If we ignore these initial columns of M', we see that the remaining columns are all linearly dependent.

The total number of equations needed to produce each linearly dependent row in M is given by the number of 1s in the corresponding column of M'. The number of equations therefore needed to generate a bias for a particular dependent row in M is one more than the number of 1s in the corresponding column of M'. The minimum value along all columns (excluding the basis elements) is deemed the lowest weight linear combination. If there is more than one column with a sum equal to the minimum, the linear combination that requires the least amount of output is the most useful.

Output: Equations needed for strongest bias.

5.5   Using Multiple Linear Approximations

Suppose that g has γ best linear approximations. Suppose the biased output equations span no more than q indices and we have an output sequence of length l which is much greater than q ($\gg q$). Then we can evaluate each output equation $l-q$ ($\approx l$) independent times using shifted subsets of the output sequence. If each of the biased equations relates to a distinct subset of output bits, then each is satisfied (or not) independently of the others, so we end up with $\gamma(l-q)$ ($\approx \gamma l$) independent evaluations in our sample instead of just $(l-q)$ evaluations. Thus we can reduce the amount of output required by a factor of γ. The amount of keystream required to distinguish a LF-NFSR with γ best linear approximations for the nonlinear update g is therefore $\frac{\gamma}{b^2}$.

6   Example Illustrating the Generalised Method

In this section we apply the method described in Sect. 5.2 to the example LF-NFSR used by Orumiehchiha et al. [32]. Note that our method identifies a stronger bias than that found in [32].

Consider a LF-NFSR of length $n = 7$, with initial state $S^0 = s_0, \ldots, s_6$, update function $g = r_0 + r_1 + r_5 + r_2 r_4 r_6$ and linear filter function $y_t = L(S^t) = r_0 + r_2 + r_3 + r_6$. In the steps described below, we only list a limited number of equations in order to save space. A total of 32 equations are needed to generate the matrix M in Sect. 6.4.

6.1   Developing System $\mathcal{L}$

The highest indexed term in L is r_6. Therefore at time $t = 0$

$$y_0 = s_0 + s_2 + s_3 + s_6$$

Rearranging this equation gives

$$s_6 = s_0 + s_2 + s_3 + y_0$$

Increasing the index of each state bit and replacing states higher than s_5 using their corresponding equations, we get the following for system $\mathcal{L}$.

$$s_6 = s_0 + s_2 + s_3 + y_0 \tag{$\mathcal{L}6$}$$

$$s_7 = s_1 + s_3 + s_4 + y_1 \tag{$\mathcal{L}7$}$$

$$s_8 = s_2 + s_4 + s_5 + y_2 \tag{$\mathcal{L}8$}$$

$$s_9 = s_3 + s_5 + s_6 + y_3 = s_0 + s_2 + s_5 + y_0 + y_3 \tag{$\mathcal{L}9$}$$

$$\vdots$$

$$s_{22} = s_0 + s_3 + s_4 + y_0 + y_2 + y_5 + y_6 + y_7 + y_8 + y_{12} + y_{13} + y_{16} \tag{$\mathcal{L}22$}$$

$$\vdots$$

6.2   Developing System $\widetilde{\mathcal{G}}$

Examining the Walsh-Hadamard Transform for g, we observe that the best linear approximation is $\widetilde{g} = r_0 + r_1 + r_5$ with bias of $\epsilon = \frac{3}{8}$. Note that all equations in system $\widetilde{\mathcal{G}}$ are probabilistic with probability $\frac{1}{2} + \frac{3}{8} = \frac{7}{8}$ of being true.

Using $\widetilde{g}$, we can develop system $\widetilde{\mathcal{G}}$, substituting state bits using system $\mathcal{L}$ where necessary. We get the following for system $\widetilde{\mathcal{G}}$:

$$s_7 = s_0 + s_1 + s_5 \tag{$\widetilde{\mathcal{G}}7$}$$

$$s_8 = s_1 + s_2 + s_6 = s_0 + s_1 + s_3 + y_0 \tag{$\widetilde{\mathcal{G}}8$}$$

$$s_9 = s_1 + s_2 + s_4 + y_1 \tag{$\widetilde{\mathcal{G}}9$}$$

$$\vdots$$

$$s_{22} = s_0 + y_0 + y_2 + y_3 + y_4 + y_6 + y_7 + y_9 + y_{11} + y_{14} \tag{$\widetilde{\mathcal{G}}22$}$$

$$\vdots$$

6.3   Developing System $\mathcal{L} + \widetilde{\mathcal{G}}$

From Steps 1 and 2 we have two systems describing the update bits in terms of the initial state bits and output bits respectively. We now add the two systems together to produce a new system. Note that system $\widetilde{\mathcal{G}}$ starts at Eq. 7. Therefore, we only use equations from system $\mathcal{L}$ that are labeled 7 or higher. Note that because system $\mathcal{L} + \widetilde{\mathcal{G}}$ is built using equations from both system $\mathcal{L}$ and system $\widetilde{\mathcal{G}}$, each equation in system $\mathcal{L} + \widetilde{\mathcal{G}}$ is probabilistic with probability $\frac{7}{8}$ of being true.

$$0 = s_0 + s_3 + s_4 + s_5 + y_1 \qquad\qquad (\mathcal{L}7 + \tilde{\mathcal{G}}7)$$

$$0 = s_0 + s_1 + s_2 + s_3 + s_4 + s_5 + y_0 + y_2 \qquad\qquad (\mathcal{L}8 + \tilde{\mathcal{G}}8)$$

$$0 = s_0 + s_1 + s_4 + s_5 + y_0 + y_1 + y_3 \qquad\qquad (\mathcal{L}9 + \tilde{\mathcal{G}}9)$$

$$\vdots$$

$$0 = s_3 + s_4 + y_3 + y_4 + y_5 + y_8 + y_9 + y_{11} + y_{12} + y_{13} + y_{14} + y_{16}$$
$$(\mathcal{L}22 + \tilde{\mathcal{G}}22)$$

$$\vdots$$

6.4   Create the Coefficient Matrix and Determine a Bias

We can create a matrix representing the coefficients of the initial state variables in system $\mathcal{L} + \tilde{\mathcal{G}}$. That is, each row in the matrix M corresponds to the state variables present in an equation in the final system. Note that $j = 6$, so the matrix M will have six columns. Note that we present M here transposed to save space.

$$M^T = \begin{bmatrix} 1&1&1&1&1&0&1&1&0&0&1&1&1&0&0&0&0&1&1&0&1&0&1&0&0&1&0&0&0&1&0&1 \\ 0&1&1&1&1&1&0&1&1&0&0&1&1&1&0&0&0&0&1&1&0&1&0&1&0&0&1&0&0&0&1&0 \\ 0&1&0&0&0&1&0&1&1&1&1&1&0&1&1&0&0&1&1&1&0&0&0&0&1&1&0&1&0&1&0&0 \\ 1&1&0&1&1&0&0&1&1&1&0&0&0&0&1&1&0&1&0&1&0&0&1&0&0&0&1&0&1&1&1&1 \\ 1&1&1&0&1&1&0&0&1&1&1&0&0&0&0&1&1&0&1&0&1&0&0&1&0&0&0&1&0&1&1&1 \\ 1&1&1&1&0&1&1&0&0&1&1&1&0&0&0&0&1&1&0&1&0&1&0&0&1&0&0&0&1&0&1&1 \end{bmatrix}$$

We find the dependent rows of M by finding a basis for the column space of M^T. This can be achieved by computing the reduced row echelon (RREF) form of M^T.

$$M' = RREF(M^T) = \begin{bmatrix} 1&0&0&0&0&0&0&1&0&1&0&1&1&1&0&1&1&0&1&0&0&0&0&0&1&0&0&1&0&1&1&1 \\ 0&1&0&0&0&0&1&0&0&0&0&0&1&1&1&1&0&0&0&1&1&1&1&1&1&1&1&1&0&0&0&0 \\ 0&0&1&0&0&0&1&0&1&1&1&1&1&0&1&1&0&0&1&1&1&0&0&0&0&1&1&0&1&0&1&0 \\ 0&0&0&1&0&0&0&0&0&1&0&0&0&0&0&0&0&1&1&1&1&0&0&0&1&1&1&1&1&1&1&0 \\ 0&0&0&0&1&0&1&0&1&0&1&0&1&1&0&0&0&1&0&1&0&0&0&0&0&1&1&1&1&0&0&1&0 \\ 0&0&0&0&0&1&1&1&1&1&1&1&1&0&0&1&1&1&1&1&1&1&1&1&1&0&0&1&0&1&1&0&0 \end{bmatrix}$$

Note that the first $j = 6$ columns in M' correspond to the basis elements and therefore have weight 1. Also observe from M' that the thirty-second column has weight 1. The position of the single 1 in the thirty-second column indicates that the first equation in system $\mathcal{L} + \tilde{\mathcal{G}}$ involves the same initial state bits are the thirty second equation.

$$0 = s_0 + s_3 + s_4 + s_5 + y_1$$

$$0 = s_0 + s_3 + s_4 + s_5 + y_0 + y_2 + y_6 + y_9 + y_{11} + y_{13} + y_{14} + y_{19} + y_{20}$$
$$+ y_{21} + y_{24} + y_{25} + y_{27} + y_{28} + y_{29} + y_{30} + y_{32}$$

A column weight of 1 is the lowest possible and so, if 32 bits of output are observed, the bias with the highest probability can be established. That is,

$$0 = y_0 + y_1 + y_2 + y_6 + y_9 + y_{11} + y_{13} + y_{14} + y_{19} + y_{20} + y_{21} + y_{24} + y_{25}$$
$$+ y_{27} + y_{28} + y_{29} + y_{30} + y_{32}$$

Two equations were used to identify this bias and so, by applying the piling up lemma, the probability of this bias being correct is given by

$$p = \Pr(E) = P(0 = y_0 + y_1 + y_2 + y_6 + y_9 + y_{11} + y_{13} + y_{14} + y_{19} +$$
$$y_{20} + y_{21} + y_{24} + y_{25} + y_{27} + y_{28} + y_{29} + y_{30} + y_{32})$$
$$= \frac{1}{2} + 2\left(\frac{3}{8}\right)^2 = 0.78125$$

NOTE: If an attacker can gain access to only a decimated version of the output sequence observed in this example, system $\mathcal{L} + \widetilde{\mathcal{G}}$ would remain the same. The attacker would simply choose to include the unknown output bits as variables in the matrix M. In doing so, the attacker is not guaranteed to obtain a linear combination of the same weight as the case when consecutive bits are observed.

7   Case Study: Grain Family

Grain is a well known family of stream ciphers that has been extensively analysed in the public literature. Grain has five main variants: Grain-V0 [21], its revised specification Grain-V1, Grain-128 [20], Grain-128a [22] and Grain-128AEAD [23]. The Grain family of stream ciphers has been extensively analysed in the public literature [1,5,10,12,25–27], which has resulted in early variants of Grain now being considered broken. More recently, a correlation attack on Grain-128a was proposed [36].

Zhang and Wang [37] note that the initialisation process of Grain allows for the possibility of an initial state containing an all zero LFSR. Zhang and Wang refer to key-IV pairs that result in such initial states as weak key-IVs. Such a weak key-IV pair effectively reduces Grain to a LF-NFSR, as the Grain LFSR is autonomous during keystream generation.

Zhang and Wang have provided distinguishing attacks on Grain-V0, Grain-V1 and Grain-128 under these conditions. In this section we will show that considering Grain under a weak key-IV as a LF-NFSR, our distinguishing attack has lower complexity than the method of Zhang and Wang for all variants after Grain-V0. We then show that our generalised distinguishing attack for regularly decimated output sequences can be directly applied to Grain-128a in both modes of operation and thus, also to Grain-128AEAD. Distinguishing Grain-128a in authentication mode or Grain-128AEAD would not be possible using Zhang and Wang's method due to the regular decimation of the output sequence.

Table 1 provides the data and time requirements for distinguishing each variant of Grain using both the method of Zhang and Wand and our new method. Based on a limited exploration of the systems $\mathcal{L} + \mathcal{G}$ (a few hundred equations in each case), our method has the same keystream and complexity requirements as Zhang and Wang's method; however, with unlimited pre-computational resources, our method has lower complexity than Zhang and Wang's for the variants beyond Grain-V0. The reason for this is that, since the keystream is not decimated, we can always obtain a combination of equations with the maximum possible bias of $2\epsilon^2$, by collecting 2^j bits of keystream. This gives a significantly lower online complexity for the attack; in the case of Grain-128a, it also has a much lower keystream requirement. It is important to note, however, that in this case the precomputation phase of the attack (determining which output bits are required for the strongest bias) will have a much higher complexity In fact, the time complexity of the precomputation will be approximately equal to the keystream requirement of 2^j. We note also that Zhang and Wang's approach does not reveal the possibility of this more efficient attack.

Table 1 highlights that distinguishing weak key-IVs for the 128-bit variants is costly in both the amount of keystream required and time complexity. In particular, we see that distinguishing Grain-128a in authentication mode requires an impractically large amount of keystream and time, much more than simply exhaustively searching the key space.

The traditional methods for distinguishing LF-NFSRs look to mitigate the nonlinear update function g by using a linear approximation $\tilde{g}$. It is common in contemporary cipher designs to choose g such that the bias between itself and any linear function is small. For instance, the nonlinear updates for Grain-128a and Grain-128AEAD have 2^{14} best linear approximations, each with a bias of less than 2^{-9}. Even for Grain-128a without authentication (which uses consecutive keystream bits for encryption), such a small bias results in a costly distinguishing attack in both time and data.

We note that the our method applied to Grain in this section may also be applicable to other stream ciphers that use a LF-NFSR, for instance our method would be directly applicable to Sprout [3]. Other ciphers with similar structures to Grain, such as Fruit [2] and Plantlet [30], ensure that the last bit of the LFSR is 1 following initialisation. This eliminates the possibility of the LFSR being initialised to the all zero state, which prevents these ciphers from operating as LF-NFSRs.

Table 1. Comparison of resource requirements when using Zhang and Wang's method [37] vs. our new method for distinguishing weak key-IVs in each variant of Grain.

Variant	No. of equations required	Bias (b)	No. of best linear approximations	Keystream required [37]	Time complexity [37]	Keystream required (new)	Time complexity (new)
Grain-V0	2	$2(\frac{164}{2^{11}})^2 \approx 2^{-6.3}$	1	$2^{12.6}$	$2^{15.7}$	$2^{12.6}$	$2^{15.7}$
Grain-V1	8	$2^7(\frac{656}{2^{13}})^8 \approx 2^{-22.2}$	1	$2^{44.3}$	$2^{47.5}$	$2^{44.3}$	$2^{47.5}$
Grain-V1	2	$2(\frac{656}{2^{13}})^2 \approx 2^{-6.3}$	1	NA	NA	2^{63}	2^{16}
Grain-128	7	$2^6(\frac{64}{2^{14}})^7 \approx 2^{-50}$	2^{14}	2^{86}	$2^{104.2}$	2^{86}	$2^{104.2}$
Grain-128	2	$2(\frac{64}{2^{14}})^2 \approx 2^{-15}$	2^{14}	NA	NA	2^{89}	$2^{33.3}$
Grain-128a (no tag)	7	$2^6(\frac{63}{2^{15}})^7 \approx 2^{-57.2}$	2^{14}	$2^{100.3}$	$2^{117.6}$	$2^{100.3}$	$2^{117.6}$
Grain-128a (no tag)	2	$2(\frac{63}{2^{15}})^2 \approx 2^{-17}$	2^{14}	NA	NA	2^{89}	$2^{37.3}$
Grain-128a (with tag)	36	$2^{35}(\frac{63}{2^{15}})^{36} \approx 2^{-289.8}$	2^{14}	NA	NA	$2^{565.6}$	$2^{583.9}$
Grain-128AEAD	36	$2^{35}(\frac{63}{2^{15}})^{36} \approx 2^{-289.8}$	2^{14}	NA	NA	$2^{565.6}$	$2^{583.9}$

Recently, a focus has been placed on lightweight cryptographic algorithms. As a result, keystream output is being limited in many modern ciphers. It therefore seems that a new general method of distinguishing LF-NFSRs is required that does not rely so heavily on finding good linear approximations of g.

8   Conclusion

This paper investigated the security of linearly filtered nonlinear feedback shift registers (LF-NFSRs) with respect to distinguishing attacks. We first formalised the method of Orumiehchiha et al. for distinguishing a LF-NFSR when consecutive bits of output are available to the attacker. We then generalised this attack to accommodate LF-NFSRs with regularly decimated output sequences, a target that cannot be attack using previous methods.

We applied the generalised distinguishing attack to the Grain family of stream ciphers. Our results highlighted that for 128-bit variants of Grain, traditional methods require vast amounts of time and data simply distinguishing when Grain is initialised using a weak key-IV. We propose that a new method of distinguishing LF-NFSRs is required in order to attack modern stream ciphers.

References

1. Afzal, M., Masood, A.: Algebraic cryptanalysis of a NLFSR based stream cipher. In: 2008 3rd International Conference on Information and Communication Technologies: From Theory to Applications, pp. 1–6. IEEE (2008)
2. Amin Ghafari, V., Hu, H.: Fruit-80: a secure ultra-lightweight stream cipher for constrained environments. Entropy **20**(3), 180 (2018)
3. Armknecht, F., Mikhalev, V.: On lightweight stream ciphers with shorter internal states. In: Leander, G. (ed.) FSE 2015. LNCS, vol. 9054, pp. 451–470. Springer, Heidelberg (2015). https://doi.org/10.1007/978-3-662-48116-5_22
4. Berbain, C., Gilbert, H., Joux, A.: Algebraic and correlation attacks against linearly filtered non linear feedback shift registers. In: Avanzi, R.M., Keliher, L., Sica, F. (eds.) SAC 2008. LNCS, vol. 5381, pp. 184–198. Springer, Heidelberg (2009). https://doi.org/10.1007/978-3-642-04159-4_12
5. Berbain, C., Gilbert, H., Maximov, A.: Cryptanalysis of grain. In: Robshaw, M. (ed.) FSE 2006. LNCS, vol. 4047, pp. 15–29. Springer, Heidelberg (2006). https://doi.org/10.1007/11799313_2
6. Coppersmith, D., Krawczyk, H., Mansour, Y.: The shrinking generator. In: Stinson, D.R. (ed.) CRYPTO 1993. LNCS, vol. 773, pp. 22–39. Springer, Heidelberg (1994). https://doi.org/10.1007/3-540-48329-2_3
7. Courtois, N.T.: Fast algebraic attacks on stream ciphers with linear feedback. In: Boneh, D. (ed.) CRYPTO 2003. LNCS, vol. 2729, pp. 176–194. Springer, Heidelberg (2003). https://doi.org/10.1007/978-3-540-45146-4_11
8. Courtois, N.T., Meier, W.: Algebraic attacks on stream ciphers with linear feedback. In: Biham, E. (ed.) EUROCRYPT 2003. LNCS, vol. 2656, pp. 345–359. Springer, Heidelberg (2003). https://doi.org/10.1007/3-540-39200-9_21
9. De Canniere, C., Preneel, B.: Trivium specifications. In eSTREAM, ECRYPT Stream Cipher Project. Citeseer (2005)

10. De Cannière, C., Küçük, Ö., Preneel, B.: Analysis of grain's initialization algorithm. In: Vaudenay, S. (ed.) AFRICACRYPT 2008. LNCS, vol. 5023, pp. 276–289. Springer, Heidelberg (2008). https://doi.org/10.1007/978-3-540-68164-9_19

11. Ding, C., Xiao, G., Shan, W. (eds.): The Stability Theory of Stream Ciphers. LNCS, vol. 561. Springer, Heidelberg (1991). https://doi.org/10.1007/3-540-54973-0

12. Dinur, I., Shamir, A.: Breaking Grain-128 with dynamic cube attacks. In: Joux, A. (ed.) FSE 2011. LNCS, vol. 6733, pp. 167–187. Springer, Heidelberg (2011). https://doi.org/10.1007/978-3-642-21702-9_10

13. Englund, H., Johansson, T.: A new simple technique to attack filter generators and related ciphers. In: Handschuh, H., Hasan, M.A. (eds.) SAC 2004. LNCS, vol. 3357, pp. 39–53. Springer, Heidelberg (2004). https://doi.org/10.1007/978-3-540-30564-4_3

14. Faugere, J.-C., Ars, G.: An algebraic cryptanalysis of nonlinear filter generators using Gröbner bases. Report, INRIA (2003)

15. Forrié, R.: The strict avalanche criterion: spectral properties of Boolean functions and an extended definition. In: Goldwasser, S. (ed.) CRYPTO 1988. LNCS, vol. 403, pp. 450–468. Springer, New York (1990). https://doi.org/10.1007/0-387-34799-2_31

16. Forré, R.: A fast correlation attack on nonlinearly feedforward filtered shift-register sequences. In: Quisquater, J.-J., Vandewalle, J. (eds.) EUROCRYPT 1989. LNCS, vol. 434, pp. 586–595. Springer, Heidelberg (1990). https://doi.org/10.1007/3-540-46885-4_56

17. Gammel, B.M., Göttfert, R.: Linear filtering of nonlinear shift-register sequences. In: Ytrehus, Ø. (ed.) WCC 2005. LNCS, vol. 3969, pp. 354–370. Springer, Heidelberg (2006). https://doi.org/10.1007/11779360_28

18. Golić, J.D., Salmasizadeh, M., Simpson, L., Dawson, E.: Fast correlation attacks on nonlinear filter generators. Inf. Process. Lett. 64(1), 37–42 (1997)

19. Hell, M., Johansson, T., Brynielsson, L.: An overview of distinguishing attacks on stream ciphers. Cryptogr. Commun. 1(1), 71–94 (2009). https://doi.org/10.1007/s12095-008-0006-7

20. Hell, M., Johansson, T., Maximov, A., Meier, W.: A stream cipher proposal: Grain-128. In: 2006 IEEE International Symposium on Information Theory, pp. 1614–1618. IEEE (2006)

21. Hell, M., Johansson, T., Meier, W.: Grain: a stream cipher for constrained environments. Int. J. Wirel. Mobile Comput. 2(1), 86–93 (2007)

22. Hell, M., Johansson, T., Meier, W.: Grain-128a: a new version of Grain-128 with optional authentication. Int. J. Wirel. Mob. Comput. 5, 48–59 (2011)

23. Hell, M., Johansson, T., Meier, W., Sönnerup, J., Yoshida, H.: Grain-128AEAD - a lightweight AEAD stream cipher. NIST Lightweight Crypt. Compet. 1 (2019)

24. Katz, J., Menezes, A.J., Van Oorschot, P.C., Vanstone, S.A.: Handbook of Applied Cryptography. CRC Press, Boca Raton (1996)

25. Khazaei, S., Hassanzadeh, M., Kiaei, M.: Distinguishing attack on grain. ECRYPT Stream Cipher Proj. Rep. 71, 2005 (2005)

26. Küçük, O.: Slide resynchronization attack on the initialization of Grain 1.0. eSTREAM, ECRYPT Stream Cipher Proj. Rep. 44, 2006 (2006)

27. Lee, Y., Jeong, K., Sung, J., Hong, S.: Related-key chosen IV attacks on Grain-v1 and Grain-128. In: Mu, Y., Susilo, W., Seberry, J. (eds.) ACISP 2008. LNCS, vol. 5107, pp. 321–335. Springer, Heidelberg (2008). https://doi.org/10.1007/978-3-540-70500-0_24

28. Massey, J.: Shift-register synthesis and BCH decoding. IEEE Trans. Inf. Theory **15**(1), 122–127 (1969)

29. Meier, W., Staffelbach, O.: Fast correlation attacks on certain stream ciphers. J. Cryptol. **1**(3), 159–176 (1988). https://doi.org/10.1007/BF02252874

30. Mikhalev, V., Armknecht, F., Müller, C.: On ciphers that continuously access the non-volatile key. IACR Trans. Symmetric Cryptol. 52–79 (2016)

31. Millan, W.: Analysis and Design of Boolean Functions for Cryptographic Applications. Doctorate (1997)

32. Orumiehchiha, M.A., Pieprzyk, J., Steinfeld, R., Bartlett, H.: Security analysis of linearly filtered NLFSRs. J. Math. Cryptol. **7**(4), 313–332 (2013)

33. Rose, G.G., Hawkes, P.: On the applicability of distinguishing attacks against stream ciphers. IACR Cryptol. ePrint Arch. **2002**, 142 (2002)

34. Rueppel, R.A.: Analysis and Design of Stream Ciphers. Springer, Heidelberg (2012). https://doi.org/10.1007/978-3-642-82865-2

35. Siegenthaler, T.: Cryptanalysts representation of nonlinearly filtered ML-sequences. In: Pichler, F. (ed.) EUROCRYPT 1985. LNCS, vol. 219, pp. 103–110. Springer, Heidelberg (1986). https://doi.org/10.1007/3-540-39805-8_12

36. Todo, Y., Isobe, T., Meier, W., Aoki, K., Zhang, B.: Fast correlation attack revisited. In: Shacham, H., Boldyreva, A. (eds.) CRYPTO 2018. LNCS, vol. 10992, pp. 129–159. Springer, Cham (2018). https://doi.org/10.1007/978-3-319-96881-0_5

37. Zhang, H., Wang, X.: Cryptanalysis of stream cipher grain family. IACR Cryptol. ePrint Arch. **2009**, 109 (2009)

A New Rabin-Type Cryptosystem
with Modulus p^2q

Digby Mooney[✉], Lynn M. Batten⑩, and Leo Yu Zhang⑩

Deakin University, Geelong, VIC, Australia
{ddmooney,lmbatten,leo.zhang}@deakin.edu.au

Abstract. In 1979, Rabin introduced a variation of RSA using the encryption exponent 2, which has become popular because of its speed. Its drawback is decryption to four possible messages which has led to various ideas to identify the correct plaintext. This paper provides a new Rabin-type cryptosystem based on a modulus of the form p^2q. Along with a theoretical proof that the decryption is correct, we provide a complete example. To demonstrate its efficiency, we compare runtime of our algorithms with those of two others with similar aims. We also conjecture that our scheme is secure against chosen ciphertext attacks because of our inclusion of Simplified Optimal Asymmetric Encryption Padding of messages.

Keywords: Rabin cryptosystem · SAEP · Correctness · Modulus

1 Introduction

In 1979, Rabin introduced a variation of RSA using the encryption exponent 2, and claimed that a signature verification based on his ideas is 'several hundred times faster than for the RSA scheme' [13]. He also proved that forging Rabin signatures is equivalent to factoring the modulus, which is a product of two prime numbers. In order to verify the signature, decryption is required and is achieved by using the Chinese Remainder Theorem (CRT) [10, Sect. 2.4.3], which in general results in four possible solutions.

1.1 Motivation and Background

Examining Rabin's scheme, Williams [17] noted that the use of special prime types would make the scheme more efficient. In particular, he used primes p and q congruent to 3 and 7 modulo 8 respectively, and restricted the message space to a certain set. While decryption still leads to four values, he was able to distinguish from these the 'correct' one by means of quadratic residue theory.

Since 1980, the Rabin scheme as adapted by Williams, has become known as the 'Rabin-Williams public-key signature scheme' which is one of the most efficient variations of RSA signature schemes known to date. In fact, in [3, Introduction], Bernstein stated: "Variants of the Rabin-Williams public-key signature

© Springer Nature Singapore Pte Ltd. 2020
L. Batina and G. Li (Eds.): ATIS 2020, CCIS 1338, pp. 61–77, 2020.
https://doi.org/10.1007/978-981-33-4706-9_5

system have, since 1980, held the speed records for signature verification." See also his comments in [1] on 'The world's fastest digital signature system' which includes data about the comparative speeds of signature checking variations using 2-adic divisibility. The Rabin-Williams scheme, sometimes referred to as the 'R-W signing technique' or the 'modular square root (MSR) technique' is still used in recent papers (as in [7] and [14] for instance) as a fast method of providing authentication, especially useful in low resourced environments.

One of the problems in using the CRT to locate square roots is that with a modulus which is a product of two primes, four square roots are always located. As mentioned in [7] and [8], the question of how to choose the correct one is an issue. Additional checking to determine the correct one is possible, and in fact was done by Williams in 1980 as mentioned above, but this leads to less efficiency in using the corresponding signature scheme. In effect, Williams [17] modified Rabin's scheme by replacing a square root by, what Bernstein [2] refers to as a 'tweaked square root', a triple which speeds up signing. Bernstein explains the reason: "Recall that Rabin's system needed to try several values of r, on average about 4 values, before finding a square congruent to Hash$(M||r)$ modulo pq." Bernstein's interpretation of the Rabin–Williams system eliminates this problem by using tweaked square roots in place of square roots.

1.2   Literature

The authors of [8] gave a comprehensive overview of the variations on Rabin's protocol along with their benefits and faults. They explained that their reason for focusing once again on the work in [13] is because of the efficiency of a simple squaring for encryption and because Rabin proved that its security is equivalent to factoring the modulus $n = pq$. They pointed out that its major drawback is the four-to-one mapping which necessitates additional work to correctly decrypt, particularly when using it as a signature scheme. Their Sect. 3 reviewed the variants of [13] based on a modulus which is a product of two primes both congruent to 3 modulo 4, including Rabin-Williams. All variants presented in that section rely on the Jacobi symbol or on Dedekind sums, use the CRT to generate four potential roots, and use additional work to determine the correct root. Section 4 of [7] examines possibilities that would extend the Rabin scheme to other types of primes. The case where $x^2 \equiv m \pmod{n}$ has no solution is considered in their Sect. 5.

In [8] the authors also attempted to solve the problem of uniquely identifying the correct root when using the CRT. They presented two ways of doing this, both using the modulus p^2q, for primes p and q with certain conditions. Nevertheless, the second method only shows probabilistic uniqueness, as a function on the bounds of p, q and the message used (see Case 1 of Proposition 3.2 of their paper). In addition, in both scenarios, their algorithms 6 and 9 need to check all four options, reducing efficiency once again. None-the-less, the use of modulus p^2q gave the current authors the idea of developing a new variation of Rabin-Williams which results, as we show in Sect. 2, in identification of the correct decryption requiring very little computation additional to the polynomial time required to find four potential solutions using the CRT.

Based on the Rabin cryptosystem, the authors of [14] provided a new authentication scheme with forward secrecy for the Industrial Internet of Things systems. In order to introduce some security, they avoided the use of a password verification table and gave a formal proof and heuristic analysis to demonstrate that their scheme provides the desired security and functional features.

1.3   Our Contributions

In this paper,we provide a new Rabin-type cryptosystem based on a modulus of the form p^2q. Along with a theoretical proof that the decryption is correct, we provide a complete example. To demonstrate its efficiency, we compare runtime of our algorithms with those of two others with similar aims. We also conjecture that our scheme is secure against chosen ciphertext attacks because of our inclusion of Simplified Optimal Asymmetric Encryption Padding of messages.

The details of our new cryptosystem scheme are given in Sect. 2. Decryption is given by Algorithm 2 followed by a theoretical proof, in Subsect. 2.4, that this decryption correctly determines the original message. For primes p and q chosen in the designated range, our proof relies on the use of the message modulo p^2q.

Message padding is an accepted necessity to ensure that short messages become sufficiently large to avoid simple attacks; it has also been developed to provide security against chosen ciphertext attacks, as described in [5]. Therefore, we enable padding of our messages as demonstrated in Sect. 3. Section 4 gives a full example of our new cryptosystem. In Sect. 5, we chose two cryptosystems with similar aims and which also employed a modulus of the form p^2q, to compare with our cryptosystem on the basis of execution time.

As we use Boneh's Simplified Asymmetric Encryption Padding (SAEP), as described in [5], to pad the message before it is encrypted, we conjecture that our scheme is secure against Chosen Ciphertext attacks. See Sect. 3 for the details.

2   Our Cryptosystem

In this section, we propose a new Rabin-type cryptosystem which we call RAMS: Rabin Alternative Modulus SAEP padded scheme. We provide a proof of correctness and a proof of unique decryption.

As usual, the scheme begins with key generation by the owner, Alice, and using her public keys, Bob chooses a message to pad, encrypt and send to her. We leave the discussion of padding to the next section, as the encryption method and parameters play an important role in it.

2.1   Key Generation

Alice chooses a security parameter k, two primes, p and q, both congruent to 3 modulo 4, and such that $2^k < p, q < 2^{k+1}$. She produces her modulus $N = p^2q$. Her public keys are N and $2^{k/2-1}$ (giving the bound $0 < m < k/2$ on the bit-length message size), private are p and q. She also chooses a hash function H

to be made public, for which the output length h is in the range $(k/2, k)$, and for use in encryption by anyone sending her an encrypted message. The hash function would be chosen from a reliable site such as [12].

2.2   Encryption

Wanting to send a message M to Alice, Bob first pads it to ensure its length falls within the required bounds. Bob acquires Alice's public parameters: modulus N, security parameter k, and hash function H and proceeds as follows. Choosing the message M of length m up to $k/2 - 1$ bits, he checks that $\gcd(M, N) = 1$. Letting the output length of H be h, he lets $s_0 = h - m$. He then chooses a random integer s_1 in the range $(\frac{3k+3}{2} - h, 2k - h)$ and a random string r of length s_1 bits. He needs to choose r such that the most significant bit of $H(r)$ is zero so that in step 7 of Algorithm 1, the most significant bit of x is the same as that of v, which is a 1. A small number of choices for r may be needed to satisfy this last requirement.

Bob now plans to construct a value of length h in order to XOR it with $H(r)$. He proceeds to set t to be a string of s_0 zeros, and set $v = M||t$ which has $m + s_0 = h$ bits. He sets $x = v \oplus H(r)$ which has h bits and $y = x||r$ which has $h + s_1$ bits and is a padded version of M (see Algorithm 3 to compare with lines of Algorithm 1).

Converting y to an integer base 10, he finally computes the ciphertext $C \equiv y^2$ $(\mathrm{mod}\ N)$ and delivers the encrypted message $(C, H(r), s_0)$ to Alice.

The entirety of steps is provided below in Algorithm 1.

Algorithm 1 - RAMS: Encryption

INPUT: The public key $(N, 2^{k/2-1})$ and hash function H with output $\{0, 1\}^h$
OUTPUT: Ciphertext triplet $(C, H(r), s_0)$
1: Choose a plaintext $M \in (0, 2^{k/2-1})$ such that $\gcd(M, N) = 1$. Let the bit-length of this plaintext be m
2: Calculate integer s_0 as $s_0 = h - m$
3: Choose $s_1 \in (\frac{3k+3}{2} - h, 2k - h)$
4: Select a random $r \in \{0, 1\}^{s_1}$ such that the most significant bit of $H(r)$ is 0
5: Set $t = \{0\}^{s_0}$
6: Set $v = M||t \in \{0, 1\}^{m+s_0}$
7: Set $x = v \oplus H(r)$
8: Set $y = x||r \in \{0, 1\}^{h+s_1}$
9: Express y as an integer in base 10
10: Compute $C \equiv y^2$ $(\mathrm{mod}\ N)$
11: Return ciphertext triplet $(C, H(r), s_0)$

Notice that in step 8, the bit-length of y is $\in (\frac{3k+3}{2}, 2k)$

2.3   Decryption

Alice receives $(C, H(r), s_0)$ from Bob and knows what each entry stands for. Since she has primes p and q and knows that C is a square in her modulus, she uses the CRT modulo pq to determine four solutions, y_1, y_2, y_3 and y_4. Of course, these pair up as negatives of each other modulo pq and any which are not in the range $(2^{\frac{(3k+3)}{2}}, 2^{2k-1})$ can be rejected. At least two will be rejected as $2^{2k-1} < \frac{pq}{2}$.

Any remaining y_i can be written as a concatenation $y_i = x_i \| r_i$, where r_i has s_1 bits and x_i has the remaining h bits. The r_i which equals Bob's r indicates the correct solution, so Alice hashes the remaining r_i's and chooses that one which has the hash $H(r)$. With negligible probability of duplicates (2^{-s_1}), there will be precisely one. For this i, compute $v_i = x_i \oplus H(r)$. Alice then writes $v_i = M_i \| t$ where t has s_0 zero bits and the remainder, M_i, has $h - s_0 = m$ bits. This remainder is the original plaintext M. The detailed algorithm is presented below.

Algorithm 2 - RAMS: Decryption

INPUT: Ciphertext triplet $(C, H(r), s_0)$, private key (p, q) and security parameter k
OUTPUT: Plaintext M

1: Compute $m_p \equiv C^{\frac{p+1}{4}} \pmod{p}$
2: Compute $m_q \equiv C^{\frac{q+1}{4}} \pmod{q}$
3: Compute two integers a and b such that $ap + bq = 1$
4: Compute $y_1 \equiv apm_q + bqm_p \pmod{pq}$
5: Compute $y_2 \equiv apm_q - bqm_p \pmod{pq}$
6: Compute $y_3 \equiv -y_2 \pmod{pq}$
7: Compute $y_4 \equiv -y_1 \pmod{pq}$
8: Reject any y_i not in the range $(2^{\frac{(3k+3)}{2}}, 2^{2k--1})$
9: View remaining y_i's as bit-strings and express as $y_i = x_i \| r_i$ with $x_i \in \{0, 1\}^h$ and $r_i \in \{0, 1\}^{s_1}$
10: For each r_i, check $H(r_i) = H(r)$
    When these are equal for r_i, continue the algorithm with x_i
11: Set $v_i = x_i \oplus H(r)$
12: Write $v_i = M_i \| t$ with $M_i \in \{0, 1\}^m$ and $t = \{0\}^{s_0}$
13: Convert string M_i from binary to base 10 and return as the decrypted plaintext.

2.4   Proof of Correctness

What is meant by the *correctness* of our algorithms is the assurance that the value we want to find in the decryption algorithm is guaranteed to be one of the four values y_i appearing in lines 4–7 of Algorithm 2. In this section we prove that this is indeed the case.

First, we require the following Lemma:

Lemma. Let $N = p^2q$. Choose $y \in Z_{pq}$. If $C \equiv y^2 \pmod{N}$ and $V \equiv C \pmod{pq}$ then $V \equiv y^2 \pmod{pq}$.

Proof. As $C \equiv y^2 \pmod{N}$, then $C = y^2 + Nk_1$ for some integer k_1. As $V \equiv C$ $\pmod{pq}$, then $V = C + pqk_2$ for some integer k_2. Combining these two equalities we find that $V = y^2 + p^2qk_1 + pqk_2 = y^2 + pq(pk_1 + k_2) = y^2 + pqk_3$ for some integer k_3. We conclude that $V \equiv y^2 \pmod{pq}$.

To prove correctness of our algorithms, it suffices to prove the next result.

Theorem. Let p and q be primes congruent to 3 modulo 4, and k a parameter such that $2^k < p, q < 2^{k+1}$. Let y be an integer such that $2^{\frac{3k+3}{2}} < y < 2^{2k-1}$. Let $C \equiv y^2 \pmod{p^2q}$. Then y is the only root of

$$C \equiv X^2 \pmod{pq}, \tag{1}$$

which is also a root of

$$C \equiv X^2 \pmod{p^2q}. \tag{2}$$

Proof. Note first that, by the Lemma, any solution to Eq. (2) is also a solution to Eq. (1), so y is a root of both.

Since p and q are congruent to 3 modulo 4, it is well known, that each of $X^2 \equiv D \pmod{q}$ and $X^2 \equiv D \pmod{p}$ has precisely two solutions. Using the CRT on Eq. (1) produces the four combinations of these solutions: y_1, y_2, y_3 and y_4 in steps 4–7 of Algorithm 2. Each y_i is a positive value less than pq, they are all distinct modulo pq and can be paired as a solution and its negative. Recalling that the initial integer y is one of these solutions, we show that it is the only one less than 2^{2k-1} which satisfies both Eqs. (1) and (2).

We work by contradiction. Suppose that two of the y_i are less than 2^{2k-1} and both satisfy (1) and (2). Say $2^{2k-1} > y_i > y_j > 2^{\frac{3k+3}{2}}$. Since $y_i^2 \equiv y_j^2 \pmod{p^2q}$, it is the case that $p^2q|(y_i - y_j)(y_i + y_j)$. We now consider three situations. Let $\alpha = 1$ or -1.

Case 1. $p^2q|(y_i - y_j)$ OR $(y_i + y_j)$
Both y_i and y_j are less than 2^{2k-1}. This bounds $|y_i \pm y_j| < 2^{2k}$. But by our assumptions on the values of p and q we find that $2^{3k} < p^2q$. This implies $p^2q \nmid (y_i - y_j)$ OR $(y_i + y_j)$.

Case 2. $pq|(y_i + \alpha y_j)$ AND $p|(y_i - \alpha y_j)$
In this situation, $p|\{(y_i + \alpha y_j) \pm (y_i - \alpha y_j)\}$ implying that $p|2y_i$ AND $p|2y_j$; since p is odd, it must divide both y_i and y_j. From the CRT, these are both linear combinations of p and q, implying that the coefficients of q in both corresponding equations are multiples of p which has a negligible chance of happening. Therefore, we can ignore this case.

Case 3. $p^2|(y_i + \alpha y_j)$ AND $q|(y_i - \alpha y_j)$
Set $(y_i + \alpha y_j) = Sp^2$, for some non-negative integer S. Then $0 \le Sp^2 \le |y_i| + |y_j|$. As each y is bounded above by 2^{2k-1}, $|y_i| + |y_j| < 2^{2k}$ while by assumption, $p^2 > 2^{2k}$. Therefore $S = 0$ and once again $y_i = \alpha y_j$ which cannot be possible for either value of α.

It follows that the original value y is the only one of the four solutions which is less than 2^{2k-1}, and which satisfies both Eqs. (1) and (2).

3   Message Padding

The authors of [6] showed that textbook Rabin and RSA are provably insecure against chosen ciphertext attacks. Therefore, to implement similar cryptosystems in a practical setting, a padding scheme that ensures security against chosen ciphertext attacks is required. Bellare and Rogaway's Optimal Asymmetric Encryption (OAEP) padding scheme [4] was developed to bridge the gap between the "practical schemes that were efficient but not well-founded and the provably-secure ones". OAEP was shown to be secure under chosen ciphertext attacks and has therefore been the standard for RSA implementation. In [5], Boneh developed a simplified version of OAEP and OAEP+ (SAEP and SAEP+ respectively). These simplified versions retain the same level of chosen ciphertext attack security as OAEP, however they only require one round of a Feistel network (hashing then XORing) while OAEP and OAEP+ require two. This simplification makes the padding scheme easier to implement and slightly more efficient. In his publication, Boneh notes that SAEP is more appropriate for use with the Rabin cryptosystem than with RSA. He writes on page 2 of [5] that "The resulting systems are better than their RSA counterparts in all aspects: (1) encryption is slightly faster, (2) the reduction given in the security proof is more efficient, and (3) security relies on the difficulty of factoring rather than the difficulty of inverting the RSA permutation".

3.1   Our SAEP Parameters

For a Rabin cryptosystem with encryption modulus N, it is only practical to select plaintexts M such that $M > \sqrt{N}$, as otherwise, $C = M^2 < N$ and any computational square root method for real numbers will recover M. Padding therefore allows for choice of plaintexts less than $\sqrt{N}$, as they can be padded to larger values.

Our padding scheme for Rabin follows the advice of Boneh and implements SAEP. (It is worth noting however that Nishioka, Satoh and Sakurai, in their $N = p^2q$ variant Rabin scheme [11], still decided to use OAEP.) Our scheme operates in the context of a known cryptosystem based on a modulus as described in the previous section.

Padding. Assume that Alice has made public her modulus N, her bound, $2^{k/2-1}$ and a hash function H whose output length is a fixed value $h \in (k/2, k)$. Bob selects a plaintext message M whose length, m, is $< k/2$. He determines $s_0 = h - m$ and takes a string t of s_0 zeros. He then chooses a random integer s_1 in the range $(\frac{3k+3}{2} - h, 2k - h)$ and a string r of length s_1 ensuring that $H(r)$ begins with a 0. This provides him with a string $v = M\|t$ of length $m + s_0$, which can be XOR'd with the hash $H(r)$ producing a length h string $x = v \oplus H(r)$. Finally, Bob takes the length $h + s_1$ string $y = x||r$ as the padded message.

Algorithm 3 - SAEP Padding

INPUT (Alice provides): Security parameter k and hash function H with output $\{0,1\}^h$
OUTPUT: Padded plaintext y

1: Select plaintext $M \in \{0,1\}^m$ such that $m < k/2$
2: Calculate integer s_0 as $s_0 = h - m$
3: Choose $s_1 \in (\frac{3k+3}{2} - h, 2k - h)$
4: Select a random $r \in \{0,1\}^{s_1}$ such that the most significant bit of $H(r)$ is 0
5: Set $t = \{0\}^{s_0}$
6: Set $v = M||t \in \{0,1\}^{m+s_0}$
7: Set $x = v \oplus H(r)$
8: Set $y = x||r \in \{0,1\}^{h+s_1}$
    Output y as the padded plaintext.

Unpadding. Bob sends y, $H(r)$ and s_0 to Alice to facilitate decryption. To unpad, Alice knows $h = m + s_0$, and so knowing $y = x||r$, based on counting digits, she calculates $s_1 = (m + s_0 + s_1) - h$. This enables her to remove r, giving her x. She then sets $v = x \oplus H(r)$ and takes t as the last s_0 zeros of this, revealing the original plaintext M from $v = M||t$. The following algorithm gives the detailed steps.

Algorithm 4 - SAEP Unpadding

INPUT: Padded plaintext y, hashed nonce $H(r)$ and integer s_0
OUTPUT: Plaintext M

1: Write $y = x||r$ with $x \in \{0,1\}^h$ and $r \in \{0,1\}^{s_1}$
2: Set $v = x \oplus H(r)$
3: Write $v = M||t$ with $M \in \{0,1\}^m$ and $t = \{0\}^{s_0}$
4: Output M as the plaintext

Chosen Ciphertext Secure Bounds. In Theorem 4 of Boneh's paper [5], he proves that under certain conditions associated with SAEP padding of Rabin cryptosystem messages, the scheme is secure against chosen ciphertext attacks. He deals with a standard modulus as a product of two primes, with security parameter k, uses a hash function with output of length h, and assumes the conditions (as in Subsects. 2.1 and 2.2) $h < k$ and $m < k/2$, where m is the bit-length of a message being padded. Note that his parameters are not the same as ours and we use a modulus of quite a different form. None-the-less, we invoke the same conditions hoping that a similar security proof could be given. We leave this for future work.

4 An Example

This example was produced using Maple software [9].

Alice's Cryptosystem. Alice begins by establishing her cryptosystem choosing $k = 129$, and the hash function MD5 with $h = 128$. She chooses primes congruent to 3 modulo 4:

$p = 12678373012324080603033928224959045 89211$ and

$q = 682192469264385070635974870208850273523$

Which sets

$N = 1096563967368292878363718859952642410110619486981968293778298856$
$23329184429311739752826776643326628232183557 0264351483.$

Alice keeps p and q private while N, k and H are public.

Bob Pads a Message Using Alice's System. Bob wants to send Alice the message $M = 11801550915596327273$ in base 10, with bit-length $m = 64$. In order to pad this to a longer message in the range $(2^{\frac{3k+3}{2}}, 2^{2k-1})$, he computes $s_0 = h - m = 64$, then produces a random nonce

$r = 666780720451107292011049724690359979194$

and checks that $H(r)$ begins with 0. The variable t is now a string of 64 zeros, leading to $v = M\|t$ being

$v = 1010001111000111100010000000011111001010110011100001100101101001$
$0000000000000000000000000000000000000000000000000000000000000000$

and $x = v \oplus H(r)$ being

$x = 1010111110111001101110111001100110101011111001011111011101000011$
$0100110011010000011101111000011010010011100100011000111001100101.$

Converting r to binary and concatenating with x yields the padded message $y = x\|r$ of $h + s_1$ bits, which he now encrypts.

Bob Encrypts the Padded Message. In base 10,

$y = 158965819957194626646313849813353024854815038324315611383947504210$
$412094950586.$

Calculating $C \equiv y^2 \pmod N$, he obtains

$C \equiv 2254806082027043180416992792665224231477298681790823884295904073 9$
$24193516599115459247569477266364517484481697 95540024.$

Bob sends $(C, H(r), s_0)$ to Alice for decryption.

Alice Decrypts the Padded Message. With her private key (p, q), Alice computes the roots of C modulo p and q as $m_p \equiv C^{(p+1)/4} \pmod{p}$ and $m_q \equiv C^{(q+1)/4} \pmod{q}$. She finds that

$m_p = 1233979000570133348142288208626848294108$ and
$m_q = 4279090097904596810782179478658573828595$.

She then uses the extended Euclidean algorithm to compute integers a and b such that $ap + bq = 1$. She finds

$a = 2933459135656099463263143805068127669 59$ and
$b = -545175897036239178260207921536398769276$.

With m_p, m_q, a and b Alice uses the Chinese Remainder Theorem to compute the four roots of C modulo pq. Namely: $y_1 \equiv apm_q + bqm_p \pmod{pq}$, $y_2 \equiv apm_q + bqm_p \pmod{pq}$, $y_3 \equiv -y_2 \pmod{pq}$ and $y_4 \equiv -y_1 \pmod{pq}$. She finds the values:

$y_1 = 82802164526350163958334783000116902477612143917940295538668351043$
$\qquad 0855734779454$,

$y_2 = 70594323919603582526881254323110332494399810239863533438510628436$
$\qquad 3616209809767$,

$y_3 = 15896581995719462664631384981335302485481503832431561138394750421$
$\qquad 0412094950586$ and

$y_4 = 36887413889728812331778563043287325022691701543547990 38237027814$
$\qquad 3172569980899$.

As the padded plaintext y was necessarily in the range $2^{\frac{3k+3}{2}} < y < 2^{2k-1}$ Alice eliminates any y_i's outside this range. In this example, y_1 and y_2 are eliminated.

Alice now performs preliminary unpadding steps on y_3 and y_4 to determine the original y. She expresses y_3 and y_4 as bit-strings and, knowing the value of h, views them as a concatenation $x_i \| r_i$ where x_i is a string of length h and r_i is a string of length s_1. In this example:

$x_3 = 10101111101110011011101110011001101010111110010111110111011010000 11$
$\qquad 01001100110100000111011110000110100100111001000110001110011001 01$,

$r_3 = 11111010110100001010010111010101110000000111100000000010011001000$
$\qquad 0101001111101111010011111010011001100110001000101000011001011 1010$,

$x_4 = 101000110001101100010010101000011010011110011010000100001001111 0$
$\qquad 10001111000110000001110010010001110011001110111100001001000011 10$

and

$r_4 = 0000011011000011001101001010010010001110100001000010101110011000$
$\qquad 10011100011010110010001001100000001110100000011110111111111100011$.

Alice now converts each r_i to base 10, computes both $H(r_i)$ and compares the result to the $H(r)$ sent by Bob. As one of y_3 and y_4 was the original padded plaintext, one of $H(r_3)$ and $H(r_4)$ will match. Alice observes that $H(r_3) = H(r)$ and consequently determines that y_3 is the original y. She continues the unpadding process with x_3.

Alice Unpads the Padded Message. Using $x = x_3$, Alice XORs x_3 with $H(r)$ to obtain v (values as above). She finds

$$v = 101000111100011110001000000001111100101011001110000110010110100100000000000000000000000000000000000000000000000000000000000000000000000000000000.$$

By removing the last s_0 zeros (equating to the t above), Alice produces the original plaintext message M.

$$M = [101000111100011110001000000001111100101011001110000110010110100l]_2$$
$$M = [11801550915596327273]_{10}$$

5 Comparative Efficiency

To contextualise RAMS in the field of public key cryptography we tested the efficiency of our cryptosystem against schemes with similar aims or structure.

5.1 Choice of Schemes for Comparison

Selection Criteria. RAMS is characterised by its rapid Rabin encryption and decryption processes: $C \equiv M^2 \pmod{N}$ for encryption and CRT for decryption. Utilising similar algorithms formed the first criterion. RAMS is also characterised by its utilisation of a modulus of the form $N = p^2q$. Thus, utilising a modulus of this kind became the second necessary criterion in scheme selection.

Schemes Tested. In addition to RAMS, we identified two other schemes which met the above criteria. They are Nishioka, Satoh and Sakurai [11] and method 2 of Mahad, Asbullah and Ariffin [8] (which is slightly faster than their method 1). Throughout this section, for brevity, we simply refer to these schemes as RAMS, NSS and MAA respectively.

5.2 Method and Materials

Computer and Software Specifications. The testing was performed on an ASUS X555UJ with an intel i5 6200U CPU @ 2.30 GHz and 8 GB Ram. The software used was Maple (version 2019.1) [9] ran on a VMware Horizon Client virtual machine (version 5.4.3 build-16346110) [16].

Terms Used. Terms and their definitions used in this section. *Security Parameter:* The term 'security parameter' refers to the value of k used to bound the primes used to construct the modulus, as in the Key Generation subsection. For a security parameter k, primes are chosen in the range $2^k < p, q < 2^{k+1}$.

Trial: A trial refers to testing conducted with a specific pair of primes for a specific security parameter. For instance, given a security parameter k, we may choose several prime pairs and run several trials.

Iteration: An iteration is a single encryption/decryption cycle within a particular trial.

Security Parameters, Primes and Trials Conducted. In our test, two security parameters were used: $k = 130$ and $k = 258$. For each value of k, three pairs of primes (congruent to 3 mod 4) were generated corresponding to trials 1, 2 and 3. Primes were generated using Maple's *rand* and *nextprime* commands. These primes are listed in Tables 1 and 2.

Each trial consisted of 1000 iterations with randomly chosen plaintexts each time. For each trial, when all iterations were complete, mean encryption and decryption speeds were calculated (see Tables 3 and 4).

To gain perspective on how each scheme performed overall, the mean encryption, decryption and total iteration times were calculated for each security parameter (see Tables 5 and 6).

The timer used for recording was the ProcessClock object intrinsic to Maple. This object records with nanosecond precision.

Algorithms and Parameters Used. Detailing the specific parameters and methods employed for each cryptosystem tested.

RAMS. In the $k = 130$ trials the hash used was MD5. In the $k = 258$ trials a hash of length greater than 129 was required. In this case a single MD5 string was duplicated (as Maple contains a very limited hash library). Of course, these methods are not cryptographically secure as MD5 has been broken [18]. However, this procedure is sufficient for testing the polynomial run-time of cryptosystems against each other.

NSS. The parameters used for the NSS trials are as follows (note that we briefly use [11]'s notation). For the $k = 130$ trials $k_0 = 128$, $k_1 = 200$ and $n = 64$ under the assumption that $|N| = 393$. Plaintexts of length 64 were chosen to ensure consistency with those chosen in the RAMS test. The hash function H was MD5 and G was a duplicated MD5 string padded with eight zeroes totalling $n + k_1 = 264$ bits. For the $k = 258$ trials, we set $k_0 = 256$, $k_1 = 391$ and $n = 129$ under the assumption that $|N| = 777$. Plaintexts of length 129 bits were used. Hash function H was a duplicated MD5 string and G was four concatenated MD5 strings padded with eight zeros totalling $n + k_1 = 520$ bits.

To decrypt, a slight modification was made to the algorithm on page 84 of [11]. This was due to a typographical error where an undefined variable (x_0) was used in that paper. We believe γ_0 was meant to be written and, when corrected, calculations for γ_1 result in four possible values rather than the two the authors suggest: $\gamma_1 \equiv (\pm y^{\frac{q+1}{4}} \pm \gamma_0)p^{-1} \pmod{q}$. In subsequent decryption steps this results in an additional four x_i's generated.

MAA. Comparing MAA with RAMS and NSS we see that the authors of the MAA paper do not employ a padding scheme in their encryption/decryption algorithms. To ensure a fair comparison in our trials, we included SAEP padding and unpadding [5] alongside MAA encryption and decryption. Hash function selection was identical to those chosen for RAMS. SAEP parameters were as follows: Choose $M \in (0, 2^{k/2-1})$ with bit-length m. Calculate s_0 as $s_0 = h - m$ where h is the bit-length of the output of the hash used. Calculate s_1 as $s_1 = 2k - m - s_0$ and select $r \in (2^{s_1-1}, 2^{s_1})$.

5.3   Results

Tables 3 and 4 display the mean encryption and decryption times over 1000 iterations for each of trials 1, 2 and 3. All times are in nanoseconds.

Tables 5 and 6 display the mean encryption, decryption and total iteration times across all three trials. All times are in nanoseconds.

The first major results to compare are the average iteration times for each security parameter (column 4, Tables 5 and 6). From $k = 130$ to $k = 258$, the mean NSS times only increase by ~ 1 ns ($53.5 \rightarrow 54.8$) and remain relatively constant while mean times for RAMS and MAA roughly double. RAMS: $16.2 \rightarrow 37.7$ and MAA: $20.7 \rightarrow 40.3$. As the security parameters have almost doubled, this computation time doubling is therefore likely to be expected. It is peculiar then that the NSS scheme remained unperturbed by the security parameter doubling. We suspect that the true iteration speed for $k = 130$ is significantly shorter than the 53.5 ns recorded. We believe this result was influenced heavily by software processing speed inconsistency (discussed in Sect. 5.4).

Table 1. Primes used for each trial with $k = 130$

$k = 130$
Trial 1 Primes
$p = 2705504114791434766693717114017724546511$
$q = 2127339908258545682831004229853465199719$
Trial 2 Primes
$p = 2544972419545419406838843306197992797347$
$q = 1561497589536265960704002876103663534979$
Trial 3 Primes
$p = 2625370090245882376902641585233542265867$
$q = 1796168108805202657285488893032989317023$

Table 2. Primes used for each trial with $k = 258$

$k = 258$
Trial 1 Primes
$p = 7942691554135091725726111722384859922078207719421798007566893$ 36458162105587063
$q = 9238681020973054691192821463385314037931755504967499692453834$ 01014875750115919
Trial 2 Primes
$p = 8458090035554651592651869856397539077232610965170025021675927$ 47113998963960419
$q = 5651204990923896048249141337511507136124940170675655774636412$ 60564095083458067
Trial 3 Primes
$p = 7886649380846385415925716570051415951674789173796846221522482$ 51347427902760179
$q = 7400059277681409306486567018034621237354646562275812773242856$ 64943078253930967

Table 3. Average performance times for each $k = 130$ trialAverage performance times for each $k = 130$ trial

$k = 130$	Enc 1	Dec 1	Enc 2	Dec 2	Enc 3	Dec 3
NSS	42.790	6.575	44.822	6.896	52.807	6.840
MAA+SAEP	16.846	3.707	16.654	3.601	16.809	4.774
RAMS	7.209	3.256	15.216	4.162	14.897	3.829

Table 4. Average performances times for each $k = 258$ trial

$k = 258$	Enc 1	Dec 1	Enc 2	Dec 2	Enc 3	Dec 3
NSS	36.711	14.68	60.348	15.101	22.131	15.536
MAA+SAEP	19.840	5.472	50.066	8.792	30.787	6.207
RAMS	31.526	8.639	35.236	8.844	21.423	7.550

Table 5. Average performance across all $k = 130$ trials

$k = 130$	Mean Enc	Mean Dec	Mean Tot
NSS	46.81	6.77	53.58
MAA+SAEP	16.74	4.02	20.76
RAMS	12.44	3.75	16.19

Table 6. Average performance across all $k = 258$ trials

$k = 258$	Mean Enc	Mean Dec	Mean Tot
NSS	39.73	15.11	54.84
MAA+SAEP	33.56	6.82	40.38
RAMS	29.39	8.34	37.73

We now compare iteration means by scheme rather than by security parameter. We see that RAMS performs 28% faster than MAA for $k = 130$ (column 4 Table 5) and 7% faster for $k = 258$ (column 4 Table 6). These results may be due to variance in virtual machine processing speed (see Sect. 5.4) but they could also be due to calculation discrepancies in the two algorithms. To identify the correct root, RAMS employs $O(n)$ hash computation [15] while MAA employs $O(n^2)$ W_i calculations. Further testing is required to determine the full effect these calculations have on the overall computation time of their systems. NSS performs worse in general compared to both RAMS and MAA. For low length keys the total time taken was >250% slower than both RAMS and MAA and for higher length keys it was still >35% slower than both (column 4 Tables 5 and 6).

We believe that the NSS scheme performed slower on average than RAMS or MAA for two reasons. The first is that NSS utilises OAEP rather than SAEP as a padding scheme. OAEP requires two feistel network rounds while SAEP only requires one. The second reason is the four additional (eight total) x_i's computed in the NSS decryption algorithm compared to RAMS and MAA that only require four. Each one of these x_i computations requires a modular squaring and division. A run-time increase is observed in the larger average decryption speeds seen in column 3 of Tables 5 and 6.

In terms of encryption, when comparing RAMS with MAA, we observe that for both key lengths and most trials the RAMS is consistently faster (Tables 3 and 4). This, however, cannot be explained by their algorithms as they both effectively utilised the same encryption methods (SAEP padding + Rabin encryption). We believe that this discrepancy could be due to the computation speed uncertainty intrinsic to the virtual machine (see Sect. 5.4). This is especially pronounced in the $k = 130$ encryption trial 1 (Table 3) where RAMS recorded an abnormally low time (7.2 ns) and in the $k = 258$ encryption trial 2 (Table 4) where MAA recorded an abnormally high time (50.1 ns). These times could be considered outliers and further testing with the same primes but without a virtual machine is required to determine whether RAMS truly performs consistently faster in encryption.

When comparing the decryption speeds of RAMS and MAA we observe that RAMS performs better at low key lengths (RAMS: 3.75 ns and MAA: 4.02 ns) while MAA performs better at the higher key length (RAMS: 8.3 4 ns and MAA: 6.82 ns). As RAMS decryption requires hash computation, perhaps computing hashes of large nonces takes significantly longer than computing $W_i = \frac{C - y_i^2}{N}$

which is required for MAA decryption. As a mathematics tool, it is possible Maple is optimised for squaring and division operations rather than hash computation. This would lead to systematically slower RAMS decryption as observed. When considering the theoretical run-time of the algorithms however we see that the complexity of hash computation is $O(n)$ [15] while the complexity of W_i computation is $O(n^2)$. This result predicts MAA to possess a slower decryption speed than RAMS as key size increases which is not seen. Given these results and this speculation, further testing with larger key lengths ($k > 258$) is needed to state anything definitive.

5.4   Sources of Uncertainty and Method Improvements

The dominant source of uncertainty in the results was the processing speed inconsistency of the virtual machine. After several hours of use, the virtual machine began to suffer significantly from lag and some computations would take up to three times as long. An effort was made to reduce this lag by restarting the virtual machine every hour in order to maintain optimal performance. However, the extent to which this enabled consistent performance is unclear and the lag is also inherently difficult to quantify. The only indicator was the positive correlation between lag and the *Memory* value at the bottom of Maple's interface. Additional analysis is required to determine exactly how this value affects computation time. For instance, is the correlation linear or nonlinear?

Multiple improvements to the method can be made if this test is conducted again. Firstly, to ensure consistent processing speed, the authors make two recommendations. A virtual machine should not be used to run the testing software and if Maple is used, an effort should be made to perform tests at similar *Memory* values. Another modification is relaxing the scheme criteria to include other notable schemes such as Rabin-SAEP, OAEP-RSA and Rabin-Williams. Researchers may also consider using key values greater than $k = 258$.

6   Conclusion

In this publication we present a new Rabin-type cryptosystem utilising an encryption modulus of the form p^2q. We provide mathematical proof that our decryption procedure correctly identifies the encrypted message. For illustrative purposes we also provide a complete example of the cryptosystem encrypting and decrypting a plaintext. We also compare the efficiency of our scheme with two other notable $N = p^2q$ schemes. We find that at low prime lengths our scheme performs at least 28% faster and at prime lengths appropriate for the transmission of a 128-bit symmetric key, it performs at least 7% faster than both. As we include a variation of SAEP in the encryption and decryption procedures, we believe that with appropriate bounds on the message space the system is chosen ciphertext secure. We leave a formal proof of security for future work.

References

1. Bernstein, D.J.: The world's fastest digital signature system (1997). http://groups. google.com/group/sci.crypt/msg/840e777ec0fc5679. Accessed 13 Oct 2020
2. Bernstein, D.J.: RSA signatures and Rabin-Williams signatures: The state of the art (2008a) . https://cr.yp.to/sigs/rwsota-20080131.pdf. Accessed 13 Oct 2020
3. Bernstein, D.J.: Proving tight security for Rabin-Williams signatures. In: Smart, N. (ed.) EUROCRYPT 2008. LNCS, vol. 4965, pp. 70–87. Springer, Heidelberg (2008b). https://doi.org/10.1007/978-3-540-78967-3_5
4. Bellare, M., Rogaway, P.: Optimal asymmetric encryption. In: De Santis, A. (ed.) EUROCRYPT 1994. LNCS, vol. 950, pp. 92–111. Springer, Heidelberg (1995). https://doi.org/10.1007/BFb0053428
5. Boneh, D.: Simplified OAEP for the RSA and Rabin functions. In: Kilian, J. (ed.) CRYPTO 2001. LNCS, vol. 2139, pp. 275–291. Springer, Heidelberg (2001). https://doi.org/10.1007/3-540-44647-8_1
6. Boneh, D., Joux, A., Nguyen, P.Q.: Why textbook ElGamal and RSA encryption are insecure. In: Okamoto, T. (ed.) ASIACRYPT 2000. LNCS, vol. 1976, pp. 30–43. Springer, Heidelberg (2000). https://doi.org/10.1007/3-540-44448-3_3
7. Elia, M., Piva, M., Schipani, D.: The Rabin cryptosystem revisited. Appl. Algebra Eng. Commun. Comput. **26**(3), 251–275 (2014). https://doi.org/10.1007/s00200-014-0237-0
8. Mahad, Z., Asbullah, M.A., Ariffin, M.R.K.: Efficient methods to overcome Rabin cryptosystem decryption failure. Malays. J. Math. Sci. **11**, 9–20 (2017)
9. Maplesoft. User Manual (2015). https://www.maplesoft.com/documentation_center/maple18/usermanual.pdf. Accessed 13 Oct 2020
10. Menezes, J., van Oorschot, P.C., Vanstone, S.A.: Handbook of Applied Cryptography, p. 68. CRC Press, Boca Raton (1997)
11. Nishioka, M., Satoh, H., Sakurai, K.: Design and analysis of fast provably secure public-key cryptosystems based on a modular squaring. In: Kim, K. (ed.) ICISC 2001. LNCS, vol. 2288, pp. 81–102. Springer, Heidelberg (2002). https://doi.org/10.1007/3-540-45861-1_8
12. NIST. Approved hash function algorithms (2020). https://csrc.nist.gov/Projects/Hash-Functions. Accessed 13 Oct 2020
13. Rabin, M.O.: Digitized signatures and public-key functions as intractable a factorization. Technical report LCS/TR-212, MIT (1979)
14. Shuai, M., Xiong, L., Wang, C., Yu, N.: A secure authentication scheme with forward secrecy for industrial internet of things using Rabin cryptosystem. Comput. Commun. **160**, 215–227 (2020)
15. Stack Overflow. Time complexity of MD5 (2017). https://stackoverflow.com/questions/43625569/time-complexity-of-md5. Accessed 13 Oct 2020
16. VMware. Vmware Horizon Client (2020). https://www.vmware.com/. Accessed 17 Oct 2020
17. Williams, H.C.: A modification of the RSA public-key encryption procedure. IEEE Trans. Inf. Theory **26**(6), 726–729 (1980)
18. Xie, T., Liu, F., Feng, D.: Fast collision attack on MD5. IACR Cryptol. ePrint Arch. **2013**, 170 (2013)

Malware Analysis Method Based Random Access Memory in Android

Wenping Ji, Jian Wang[✉], Xudong He, and Jiqiang Liu

Beijing Key Laboratory of Security and Privacy in Intelligent Transportation,
Beijing Jiaotong University, Beijing, China
wangjian@bjtu.edu.cn

Abstract. Mobile phone has become an indispensable part of people's life, and an increasing number of information is stored on the mobile phones, once malware infects your phone that will cause serious damage to your personal and property security. The study of malicious software has been proposed constantly, but with so many applications flooding into marketplace and the improvement of malicious software, there are still some gaps in software quality control. The continuous improvement of malware also requires us to improve the detection technology in real time, and more importantly, we need to find more characteristics of malware on various aspects. This article will focus on the dynamic characteristics of malware and aim at random access memory in Android to carry out the experiment. Random access memory is the memory that application needs to reside while it is running, and it is a good reflection of the running characteristics of apps. Hence we extract the random access memory of software and analyse it on the process dimension, rather than on the analysis of the memory block. And the main experiment structure of our method is convolutional neural network. Based on our research, we found the relationship between malware and some process that can be used to effectively classify malware. The experiment result shows that this method has greatly improved the accuracy on the detection of malware.

Keywords: Mobile · Security · Malware · Process

1 Introduction

The development of technology makes more and more people go online, in 2019, 4.54 billion people had access to the Internet, accounting for nearly 60% of the world's population. According to the 2019 global mobile Internet user behavior guide released by the APUS research institute [1], smartphone users spend 5.4 h per day on their mobile device in average, with mobile applications, such as video, games and online shopping, becoming the top time killer. It is referred in the 2020 mobile market report released by App Annie in the US, the number of app downloads reached 204 billion in 2019, an increase of 6% from 2018. The emergence of a large number of users and apps also makes the malware more active.

Kaspersky antivirus software detected 3,503,952 malicious installation packages, 69,777 new mobile banking trojans, 68,362 new mobile blackmail trojans in 2019 [2].

© Springer Nature Singapore Pte Ltd. 2020
L. Batina and G. Li (Eds.): ATIS 2020, CCIS 1338, pp. 78–94, 2020.
https://doi.org/10.1007/978-981-33-4706-9_6

It's worth noting that there are two major trends: attackers attack users' personal data more frequently, and trojans are detected more frequently in the app market. What's more, malware developers not only generated more software packages, but also improved their technology, especially to bypass the limitations of operating systems. For example, for the sake of battery savings, Android places restrictions on the background operations of applications, which have a negative impact on adware. To get around these limitations, KeepMusic adware doesn't request permission like malware, and the program starts looping silently to play an MP3 file. When the operating system finds that the music player is running, it does not terminate the KeepMusic background process. Improvements in technology make malware more difficult to detect and remove.

Currently, many methods have been proposed for malware detection. Arora et al. [3] combined network traffic and system permissions, and proposed a method to classify malware by using FP-growth algorithm to generate frequent patterns. Alswaina et al. [4] focused on the permission of software and simplified permission dataset by extremely randomized trees. Ma et al. [5] constructed a control flow diagram (CFG) using source code, and then builds three different types of application programming interface (API) data sets based on the CFG: Boolean datasets, frequency datasets, and chronological datasets. Three detection models were constructed based on each data set: API usage detection model, API frequency detection model and API sequence detection model, and the final results were obtained by combining the three models. Zhang et al. [6] proposed a flexible framework to use n-gram analysis and feature hashing to extract multilevel fingerprints from the application's XML, DEX, APK and other files and train the classifier in parallel. Innovative framework proposed by Kim et al. [7] build a multimodal deep neural network model to reflect various characteristics of applications in various aspects. This framework relies on multiple static features for detection, but more features can be expanded if needed.

With the development of technology, malware becomes more concealed, more difficult to detect and even more harmful. Old malware is being eliminated and new malware is developing, which also requires us to improve the research method of malware detection accordingly, and to study the characteristics of malware from more aspects. So we choose random access memory (RAM) as our starting point. Programs will leave traces in RAM when they run, so we propose a new method of studying malware which deeply analyzes the memory, pays attention to the impact of malware on some system processes, and identifies malware from the process dimension. The contribution of our work is depicted as follows:

- We propose a new method for malware analysis that exploits the differences in malware performance between different processes, and the experiment achieves good result.
- We deeply analyze the experimental results and find that the detection rate of malware has relationship with their own behavior on process. Then we analyse the malware behavior in details, and provide the new idea for the future work.

The rest of the paper is organized as follows: Sect. 2 explains the related work of malware detection. Section 3 theoretically depicts the background knowledge of our method, and the method details explained in Sect. 4. Section 5 shows the experiment and result of our method, and followed by Sect. 6 that reviews and draws a conclusion of our research.

2 Related Work

Currently, the methods of malware recognition are various and contain many aspect of malware, such as API call, permission, network traffic, memory and so on. This section will review some malware detection methods based on these features.

2.1 Method Based on Memory

In the memory aspect, Xu et al. [8] proposed a hardware-assisted malware detection framework, they use the difference of memory access patterns to classify malware. Rathnayaka [9] draw support from the memory forensic analysis to detect malware. In order to decrease the encryption, obfuscated or packed nature in malware samples, static analysis was also performed on malware in this work. Studies have shown that successful malware infections leave footprints in memory. The work of [10, 11] also used the memory analysis as the basis of classification. Dai et al. [12] proposed a method to convert the memory into a fixed-size grayscale image, and then leverage the feature extracted by HOG to classify the malware. Tang et al. [13] took the hardware performance counter as the key of malware exploitation detection, but they are aimed at Windows. In the work of Kanad [14], they monitored the HPC periodically to collect data and theoretically analyzed the probabilities of HPC-based malware detection. Dump memory and extract memory features are the method of [15, 16]. This traditional methods can be more specific on what characteristics malware behaves differently from normal software, but feature selection requires more attention.

2.2 Method Based on Permission

In the permission aspect, Kandukuru et al. [17] extracted the list of permissions requested by the application from androidmanifest.xml file and transformed permissions into vector. This is a common approach to process permissions. The traffic features extracted from TCP conversation was combined with permission vector. Veelasha M. et al. [32] proposed a contrast permission pattern mining algorithm to identify the interesting permission sets. The permissions included not only required permissions, but also used permissions, that's one of the differences with this job. Experiments showed that these combined permission sets were valid.

2.3 Method Based on Traffic

In the network traffic aspect, Hernandez et al. [18] used the traffic features and power consumption characteristic to do the contrast experiment. Neutral network and URLs visited by application was combined in [19]. The URLs was performed text-like segmentation and skip-gram algorithm in word2vect was took to train the vector representation. AlAhmadi et al. [20] reassembled the network flow traces to conn logs and encoded the flow to generate malware profiles. Wang et al. [21] used one-dimensional convolution neural networks to classify end-to-end encrypted traffic. Automatically learn was also used to omit some traditional steps, such as features design, features extraction and features selection.

2.4 Method Based on API Call

In the API call aspect, Su et al. [22] proposed a deep learning method that combined features including sensitive API calls, requested permission, used permission, action, app component with deep belief networks. A feature-hybrid malware variants detection approach proposed by Zhang et al. [23] integrated opcodes features and API call features to improve the malware detection precision. Maldozer et al. [31] proposed a method combines deep learning and raw sequence of API method calls to detect Android malware. Their method also had a good effect. The difference between us is that we pick different features. That is to say, we are analyzed from the aspects of different malware. A comprehensive analysis of malware can be considered from several aspects of software in the future.

2.5 Other Method

Malware visualization is popular among the methods of identifying malware [24–27]. RGB-colored image converted by malware is used in [28], except for the features extracted from the RGB-colored images, some local features acquired from code and data sections was also combined to distinguish malware. The RGB-colored images can contain more information about malware, that is also an area worthy of further study in the future.

Though analyzing malware based on memory has already been done, we've chosen a new perspective to analyze memory. In this paper, we take an in-depth look at the performance of malware on memory, not analyze the entire memory, but the performance of malware on the process. We start from the process differences to analyze the different performance of malware and normal software.

3 Background Knowledge

In order to have a better understanding of our methods, this chapter mainly introduces some background knowledge about our method.

3.1 RAM

RAM is the memory in which the phone runs apps, all apps need to be resident when they run, and it is a good reflection of the running characteristics of apps. Malware must cause some changes in RAM during run time, so we extracted the RAM of the program while it was running. Table 1 shows the details of RAM features.

Table 1. RAM features

Name	Description
Native Heap	Memory allocated using malloc in Native Code
Dalvik Heap	Memory allocated by the Dalvik virtual machine, not including its own expenses
Dalvik Other	Memory occupied by class data structures and indexes
Stack	Stack memory
Cursor	Memory occupied by CursorWindow, related to SQL
Ashmem	Anonymously Shared memory
Other dev	Memory occupied by internal Driver
.so mmap	Memory occupied by mapped .so code
.jar mmap	Memory consumed by Java file code
.apk mmap	Memory consumed by apk code
.ttf mmap	Memory occupied by TTF file code
.dex mmap	Memory occupied by mapped dex code
Other mmap	Memory occupied by other files

3.2 Convolution Neutral Network Model

So far, many researches about applying convolutional neural networks have been published. Convolutional Neural Networks (CNN) is a type of feedforward neural networks that includes convolution calculations and possesses deep structure. It is one of the representative algorithms of deep learning. CNN can shift-invariably classify input information according to its hierarchical structure so that it plays an important role in image classification and other domains. Therefore, CNN is suitable for our experiment. In the model training phase, we took convolutional neutral network to train our model.

Convolutional neutral network contains convolutional layer, pooling layer and fully connected layer. In convolutional layer, network carries on the characteristic graph computation with a set of learnable filters. CNN slide each filter across the width and height of the input volume and compute dot products between the entries of the filter and the input at any position. Suppose the size of image is H * W * D, the size of a filter is K * K * D, and the number of filters is N. The stride is S refers that we move the filters S pixel at a time. Each filter produces a feature map and these feature maps will stack along the depth direction. The size of output feature map is

$$F = ((H - K + 2P)/S + 1, \quad (W - K + 2P)/S + 1, D) \tag{1}$$

P stands for padding size, whether to add 0 to the edge of the input image matrix. Adding padding makes the input and output dimensions of the convolution layer consistent. In general, when the strides is 1, the padding sets to be

$$P = (K - 1)/2 \tag{2}$$

The function of pooling layer is to increasingly reduce the spatial size and decrease the amount of parameters. Adding pooling layers also prevent overfitting. In general, a pooling layer often takes filters of size 2 * 2 so that both the width and the height are reduced by 2. And the pooling layer does not affect the depth dimension. There are max pooling and average pooling, we choose max pooling to reduce the computation parameters.

The fully connected layer combines all local features into global features to calculate the score for each final category. That is the biggest difference between fully connected layer and convolutional layer, whether neurons are full connected to all activations in the previous layer.

3.3 Evaluation

The experiment takes precision rate and recall rate as the indicators of measure the effect of classification. Precision rate refers to the quantity of correct sample which is classified correct in all predicted sample and recall rate refers to the quantity of sample that can be detected in all correct sample. The calculation of precision and recall are as follows:

$$Precision\ rate = TP/(TP + FP) \qquad (3)$$

$$Recall\ rate = TP/(TP + FN) \qquad (4)$$

TP refers to true positive, is the number of samples belong to positive that labeled as positive. FP represents false positive, is the number of samples belong to negative but labeled as positive. TN refers to true negative, is the number of samples belong to negative that labeled as negative. FN represents false negative, is the number of samples belong to positive that labeled as negative.

4 Methodology

In the previous section we introduced our background knowledge, in this section we will talk about our methods. Mobile phone programs run in the random access memory and different applications have different memory behavior. So we investigated the memory performance of different kinds of software. But instead of analyzing all the memory, we extract memory characteristics of some processes and transform the values into images. Then use the advantages of CNN to classify these images, that is, to classify the software. Figure 1 shows the framework of our method.

4.1 Process Analyze Phase

Adware. An adware is a program installed without a user's consent or knowledge during the install of another program. Adware is also called "pitchware", it regularly collects users' browsing behaviors in order to pop up targeted advertisements on the computer. Some adware works more on the browser. When the user uses the browser, the malicious software will load the web page with various ads in the browser, continuously display the

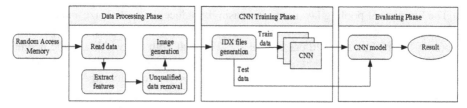

Fig. 1. The framework of our method.

ads, and even pop up the page when the user stays on the Android main interface. In addition to displaying ads, the malware redirects URLs to other malicious sites, sometimes changes the user's browser settings without the user's knowledge. Some adware may ask the user to install incorrect software updates or hand over sensitive personal information. What's more, malware can steal user's login data, then access to Gmail, Google photo albums and Google play by upgrading their permissions. Such as Gooligan, after getting root access, downloads a new malicious module from a C&C server and installs it on an infected device. This module injects code into running Google Play or GMS (Google mobile service) to mimic user behavior, so Gooligan can avoid detection. This module allows Gooligan to: Steal user's Google email account and authentication token information; Install and score apps from Google Play to improve reputation; Install adware to generate revenue. The attackers behind Shuanet, Shedun and Kemoge would repackage legitimate applications, including Facebook, Twitter, WhatsApp and other popular apps, inject malicious code and then redistribute it to third-party app stores.

Ransomware. Ransomware is a malicious program that infects a computer and then locks some part of it, preventing the user access to their computer or data. Commonly, after the ransomware is loaded onto the user's device, a message is displayed demanding payment to unlock it. Ransomware varies in its degree of difficulty to remove, as well how many areas are locked, ranging from a few files to the entire hard drive. Ransomware is also known as a "cryptovirus" or "cryptotrojan" and there are three forms of ransomware: first, by setting the touch feedback of the touch screen or virtual keys of the phone as invalid, the smartphone cannot enter other interfaces by touching; second, frequently forced to top a specified page, resulting in the phone can't switch applications; third, change the phone unlock password so that the user cannot unlock the phone. And the operation that most ransomware cannot avoid is to need to traverse the disk file and display the full screen. In details, Jisut also changes the wallpaper of the device or plays sounds in the background. Pletor will pretend to be a media player for watching videos from the site and will display images taken by the smartphone's front-facing camera to warn the victim. Svpeng also tries to get users' bank card details by displaying its own window at the top of the Google Play app.

Scareware. Scareware may claim to find threats on device merely to scare the user into purchasing a solution, such as antivirus, registry cleaner or some other software that repairs problems or enhances performance. Scareware is also called "fake antivirus" and "rogue antivirus". A warning message that pops up from a website that claims the user's computer is currently contaminated or not running properly. As an example of scareware, FakeAV usually pretends to scan the computer and look for nonexistent threats, sometimes it creates files full of junk and then detects them.

SMS Malware. SMS malware usually sends messages without the user's knowledge to subscribe to some paid content and so on. It collects the user's SMS, phone calls, browsing history, bookmarks, runtime logs, etc. Some malware even steals the user's personal information and sends it to a remote server. For example, FakeNotify is an advanced messaging Trojan and it is disguised as an update notification program. When the user clicks the button to proceed with the "download", the malware will send three sets of SMS message immediately.

Therefore, based on the analysis of malware behavior and the statistics of the process, we can find some processes are closely related to malware. Such as systemui, which is the system process for the Android system status bar and a set of UI components for system-level information display and interaction provided by the system to users. Systemui contains notification, keyguard, volumeUI and so on, which are used intimately by malware. So combine with the behavior of malware, we have selected 12 processes from the frequently occurring processes, including "com.android.chrome", "com.google.android.gms", "com.google.propress .gapps", "android.process.media", "xyz.klinker.messager", "com.facebook.katana", "com.google.android.inputmethod.latin", "com.android.phone", "com.android.nfc ", "com.google.android.googlequicksearchbox:interactor", "com.android.systemui", "system". The followed malware analysis is based on the 12 processes. Some details show in Table 2.

4.2 Data Processing Phase

This phase is the process of data. In this phase, the all.RamUsage file of software are collected by python script and sorted by their category. Then the corresponding process and memory feature values described in the third section are extracted. The output form is defined as a set $R = \{P1, P2, \cdots P12\}$, and P stands for the twelve process, is a set $P = \{f_1, f_2, \cdots f_n\}, f$ refers to ram feature. Next step, save the extracted features as csv file, clean the data and remove the unqualified data. Then normalize the data and convert the extracted feature values into grayscale images. The method of converting feature into grayscale is depicted in Table 3. Considering the number of feature values, we finally converted the data into images of size 28 * 28. Figure 2 shows the example of converted images of malware.

4.3 CNN Training Phase

In this phase, we transform the grayscale converted by memory features to IDX file, for convenient to convolution network. The algorithm of converting grayscale is given in Table 4. Then split the data into train data and test data. Use the train data to generate CNN model and the CNN architecture is used in both binary classification and category classification. All the images are reshaped into a size of 28 * 28 * 1 (1 stands for the channel depth) and ReLu function was selected as activation function. Choose cross-entropy function as the loss function. Our CNN framework is shown in Fig. 3.

Table 2. The process we choose

Process	Introduction
com.android.chrome	Chrome browser
com.google.android.gms	Google Mobile Service, including Google maps, Gmail, YouTube and more
com.google.process.gapps	Google's proprietary application set
android.process.media	Android media store process
xyz.klinker.messenger	Pulse application
com.facebook.katana	Facebook
com.google.android.inputmethod.latin	Input method
com.android.phone	The package name of the system phone application for Android
com.android.nfc	NFC
com.google.android.googlequicksearchbox:interactor	Google quicksearchbox
com.android.systemui	Android system interface, including status bar, navigation bar, screenshot and so on
system	The core running process of the phone, including resource allocation, CPU distribution, etc.

Table 3. Algorithm of converting RAM features

Algorithm   RAM features converted to grayscale
Input: RAM feature csv file
Output: ImageFile
1): **function** ToImage (RAM feature csv file)
2):   normalize the RAM feature csv file
3):   **for** row in RAM feature csv file **do**
4):   transform row in csv file into grayscale
5):   insert grayscale to ImageFile
6):   **end for**
7): **end function**

4.4   Evaluating Phase

We use the test data to evaluate the model built in the CNN training phase. Make comparison with other's work and other traditional method. Finally, further analysis about the result is made.

Fig. 2. Converted images of malware.

Table 4. Algorithm of converting grayscale images

Algorithm   Grayscale converted to IDX file
Input: ImageFile
Output: IDX file
1): **function** ToIDX (ImageFile)
2):   split the ImageFile into training set and testing set
3):   transform the images of training set to IDX3 file
4):   transform the labels of training set to IDX1 file
5):   transform the images of testing set to IDX3 file
6):   transform the labels of testing set to IDX1 file
7): **end function**

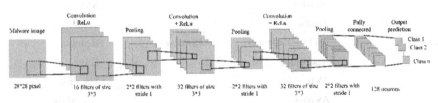

Fig. 3. CNN framework.

5   Experiment

5.1   Experiment Setup

Our programs are written in Python. The base experiment environment is a 64-bit Windows 10, with the CPU of Intel(R) Core(TM) i5-8250U @1.60 GHZ and 8 GB installed memory. The convolution network runs on Ubuntu 16.04 64 bit OS. A GPU of Nvidia GeForce GTX 1080Ti was applied to accelerate the training. The dataset we used is CICInvesAndMal2019 [29], proposed by the Canadian Institute for Cybersecurity. It contains 426 malwares that come from 42 malware families and 5, 065 benign apps collected from Google play market published in 2015, 2016, 2017. The reasons why we choose this dataset are as follows: firstly, this dataset is captured based on the real environment (Google pixel phone), including traffic, memory, logs, permissions, API calls, etc., and there are many scenes of malicious software activation [30]; secondly, it has a reasonable balanced number between malicious and benign samples in the android datasets; thirdly, the dataset contains new sample of diverse malware and includes 4 malware categories (adware, ransomware, scareware, SMS malware) and 42 malware families of malware (The malware family details is given in Table 5.). We selected the memory data captured immediately after the installation of the malicious software (1–3 min) as our experiment data. Then, through the data processing to generate the normalize data and send the data to train model. The experimental process is shown in Fig. 4.

Table 5. Malware contained in dataset

Malware category	Malware family	Malware category	Malware family
Adware	Dowgin	Ransomware	Charger
	Ewind		Jisut
	Feiwo		Koler
	Gooligan		Lockpin
	Kemoge		Pletor
	Koodous		PornDroid
	Mobidash		RansomBO
	Selfmite		Simplocker
	Shuanet		SVpeng
	Youmi		WannaLocker
Scareware	AndroidDefender	SMSmalware	Beanbot
	AndroidSpy.277		Biige
	AVforAndroid		Fakeinst
	AVpass		FakeMart
	FakeAPP		FakeNotify
	FakeApp.AL		Jifake
	FakeAV		Mazarbot
	FakeJobOffer		Nandrobox
	FakeTaoBao		Plankton
	Penetho		SMSsniffer
	VirusShield		Zsone

5.2   Evaluate

In order to better test the performance of our method, we adopted a variety of comparison methods.

Comparison with Other's Work. The experiment results show that our method has achieved good results in both binary and category classification, and the accuracy is

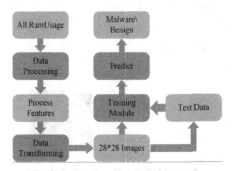

Fig. 4. The process of RAM experiment.

above 90%. Compared to L. Taheri's method of combining API calls and traffic flows, our method improves the precision of malware category classification by about 10%, the accuracy of malware binary classification up 7%. Compared with L. Taheri's previous method, we improved the binary classification accuracy of 14% and category classification accuracy of 40%. Table 6 shows our experimental results. Figure 5 depicts the comparison between our method with L. Taheri's method.

Table 6. Experiment results

Classification	Precision	Recall
Binary	99.73%	99.73%
Category	90.23%	90.53%

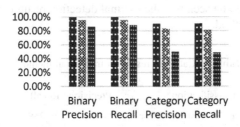

Fig. 5. The comparison of result with other's method.

In order to contrast, we also converted the traffic data into images. We used the traffic pcap files of malware and converted byte to pixel in image. Then use these images to train the model. This experiment is shown in Fig. 6. The result is given in Fig. 7. The horizontal axis represents the size of the transformed image. The picture shows that our method is more improved than the method of transforming traffic into images.

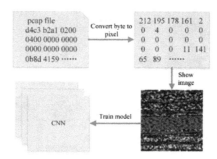

Fig. 6. The process of traffic experiment.

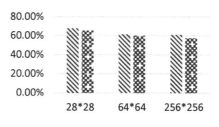

Fig. 7. The result of traffic visulization. (The horizontal axis represents the size of the transformed image.)

Comparison with Traditional Work. In addition to the method of image conversion, we also used traditional method such as K-Nearest Neighbor, Support Vector Machine, Logistic Regression, Decision Tree and Random Forest for comparison, the result is shown in Table 7. It can be seen that the optimal detection result can reach 82.5%, but it is lower than our method.

Table 7. Category results of traditional method

Classification	Precision	Recall
K-Nearest Neighbor	64.00%	59.25%
Support Vector Machine	68.75%	67.50%
Logistic Regression	64.75%	61.25%
Decision Tree	75.60%	74.50%
Random Forest	82.50%	81.75%

5.3   Result Analysis

The confusion matrix of category classification is given in Fig. 8. Further analysis of the experiment shows that SMS malware is the easiest to detect, followed by ransomware, while scare malware and adware are the most difficult to detect. This is inseparable from the characteristics of ransomware, which makes it impossible for a smartphone to enter other interfaces by touching a part of the phone's touch screen or the touch feedback of a virtual key by setting it as invalid. Ransomware also forces the phone to frequently place a specified page at the top, making it impossible for the phone to switch applications properly. The operation that most ransomware can't avoid is the need to traverse disk files. These behavioral characteristics make them easier to detect. FakeApp (belong to Scareware) and Selfmite (belong to Adware) is very similar to benign software. All of these reasons may cause errors in the detection.

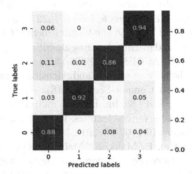

Fig. 8. Confusion matrix of category classification. (0: Adware, 1: Ransomware, 2: Scareware, 3: SMSmalware)

6   Conclusion

Continuous improvement of malicious software requires the more aspects we should analyse about the malicious software. In this article, we proposed a new method based on RAM to detect malicious software, the analysis of the previous methods tend to extract large amounts of memory, analyze malware from the memory block. Because of the discontinuity of the memory, it is wasteful to extract a large amount of memory, also can add some noise to the experiment. Therefore, according to the behavior of the malware analysis, we selected the fixed threads, on the basis of these threads, the malicious software RAM was converted into image, then combined with convolution neutral network to classify the malware. The experimental results show that this method is feasible and get good result in the classification. However, through experiments, we also found that there is still some room for improvement in using RAM to distinguish between adware and ransomware. In the next step, we will further analyse the reason and ameliorate our method to improve the accuracy of the classification of adware and ransomware.

Acknowledgements. This work was supported in part by the Natural Science Foundation of China under Grants 61672092, in part by the Fundamental Research Funds for the Central Universities of China under Grants 2018JBZ103, Major Scientific and Technological Innovation Projects of Shandong Province, China (No. 2019JZZY020128).

References

1. 360 Core Security Blog. https://blogs.360.cn/post/review_android_malware_of_2019.html
2. Mobile malware summary report in 2019. https://www.freebuf.com/articles/terminal/228295.html
3. Arora, A., Peddoju, S.K.: NTPDroid: a hybrid android malware detector using network traffic and system permissions. In: 17th IEEE International Conference on Trust, Security and Privacy in Computing and Communications/12th IEEE International Conference on Big Data Science and Engineering (TrustCom/BigDataSE), New York, NY, pp. 808–813 (2018)
4. Alswaina, F., Elleithy, K.: Android malware permission-based multi-class classification using extremely randomized trees. IEEE Access **6**, 76217–76227 (2018)
5. Ma, Z., Ge, H., Liu, Y., Zhao, M., Ma, J.: A combination method for android malware detection based on control flow graphs and machine learning algorithms. IEEE Access **7**, 21235–21245 (2019). https://doi.org/10.1109/ACCESS.2019.2896003
6. Zhang, L., Thing, V.L.L., Cheng, Y.: A scalable and extensible framework for android malware detection and family attribution. Comput. Secur. (2018)
7. Kim, T., Kang, B., Rho, M., Sezer S., Im, E.G.: A multimodal deep learning method for android malware detection using various features. IEEE Trans. Inf. Forensics Secur. **14**(3), 773–788 (2019). https://doi.org/10.1109/tifs.2018.2866319
8. Xu, Z., Ray, S., Subramanyan, P., Malik, S.: Malware detection using machine learning based analysis of virtual memory access patterns. In: Design, Automation & Test in Europe Conference & Exhibition (DATE), Lausanne, pp. 169–174 (2017). https://doi.org/10.23919/date.2017.7926977
9. Rathnayaka, C., Jamdagni, A.: An efficient approach for advanced malware analysis using memory forensic technique. In: IEEE Trustcom/BigDataSE/ICESS, Sydney, NSW, pp. 1145–1150 (2017)
10. Brengel, M., Rossow, C.: MemScrimper: time- and space-efficient storage of malware sandbox memory dumps. In: Giuffrida, C., Bardin, S., Blanc, G. (eds.) DIMVA 2018. LNCS, vol. 10885, pp. 24–45. Springer, Cham (2018). https://doi.org/10.1007/978-3-319-93411-2_2
11. Javaheri, D., Hosseinzadeh, M.: A framework for recognition and confronting of obfuscated malwares based on memory dumping and filter drivers. Wirel. Pers. Commun. **98**(1), 119–137 (2017). https://doi.org/10.1007/s11277-017-4859-y
12. Dai, Y., Li, H., Qian, Y., Lu, X.: A malware classification method based on memory dump grayscale image. Digit. Invest. **27**, 30–37 (2018). https://doi.org/10.1016/j.diin.2018.09.006
13. Tang, A., Sethumadhavan, S., Stolfo, S.J.: Unsupervised anomaly-based malware detection using hardware features. In: Stavrou, A., Bos, H., Portokalidis, G. (eds.) RAID 2014. LNCS, vol. 8688, pp. 109–129. Springer, Cham (2014). https://doi.org/10.1007/978-3-319-11379-1_6
14. Basu, K., Krishnamurthy, P., Khorrami, F., Karri, R.: A theoretical study of hardware performance counters-based malware detection. IEEE Trans. Inf. Forensics Secur. **15**, 512–525 (2020). https://doi.org/10.1109/TIFS.2019.2924549
15. Milosevic, J., Ferrante, A. and Malek, M.: What does the memory say? Towards the most indicative features for efficient malware detection. In 13th IEEE Annual Consumer Communications & Networking Conference (CCNC), Las Vegas, NV, pp. 759–764 (2016). https://doi.org/10.1109/ccnc.2016.7444874

16. Milosevic, J., Malek, M., Ferrante, A.: A friend or a foe? Detecting malware using memory and CPU features. In: Proceedings of the 13th International Joint Conference on e-Business and Telecommunications (ICETE 2016): SECRYPT, vol. 4, pp 73–84 (2016). https://doi.org/10.5220/0005964200730084

17. Kandukuru, S., Sharma, R.M.: Android malicious application detection using permission vector and network traffic analysis. In: 2nd International Conference for Convergence in Technology (I2CT), Mumbai, pp. 1126–1132 (2017). https://doi.org/10.1109/i2ct.2017.8226303

18. Hernandez Jimenez, J., Goseva-Popstojanova, K.: Malware detection using power consumption and network traffic data. In: 2nd International Conference on Data Intelligence and Security (ICDIS), South Padre Island, TX, USA, pp. 53–59 (2019). https://doi.org/10.1109/icdis.2019.00016

19. Wang, S., et al.: Deep and broad learning based detection of android malware via network traffic. In IEEE/ACM 26th International Symposium on Quality of Service (IWQoS), Banff, AB, Canada, pp. 1–6 (2018). https://doi.org/10.1109/iwqos.2018.8624143

20. AlAhmadi, B.A., Martinovic, I.: MalClassifier: malware family classification using network flow sequence behaviour. In: APWG Symposium on Electronic Crime Research (eCrime), San Diego, CA, pp. 1–13 (2018). https://doi.org/10.1109/ecrime.2018.8376209

21. Wang, W., Zhu, M., Wang, J., Zeng, X., Yang, Z.: End-to-end encrypted traffic classification with one-dimensional convolution neural networks. In: IEEE International Conference on Intelligence and Security Informatics (ISI), Beijing, pp. 43–48 (2017). https://doi.org/10.1109/isi.2017.8004872

22. Su, X., Zhang, D., Li, W., Zhao, K.: A deep learning approach to android malware feature learning and detection. In: IEEE Trustcom/BigDataSE/ISPA, Tianjin, pp. 244–251 (2016). https://doi.org/10.1109/trustcom.2016.0070

23. Zhang, J., Qin, Z., Yin, H., Ou, L., Zhang, K.: A feature-hybrid malware variants detection using CNN based opcode embedding and BPNN based API embedding. Comput. Secur. **84**, 376–392 (2019). https://doi.org/10.1016/j.cose.2019.04.005

24. Wang, Y., An, J., Huang, W.: Using CNN-based representation learning method for malicious traffic identification. In: IEEE/ACIS 17th International Conference on Computer and Information Science (ICIS), Singapore, pp. 400–404 (2018)

25. Wang, W., Zhu, M., Zeng, X., Ye, X., Sheng, Y.: Malware traffic classification using convolutional neural network for representation learning. In: International Conference on Information Networking (ICOIN), Da Nang, pp. 712–717 (2017). https://doi.org/10.1109/icoin.2017.7899588

26. Sun, G., Qian, Q.: Deep learning and visualization for identifying malware families. IEEE Trans. Depend. Secure Comput. 1 (2018). https://doi.org/10.1109/tdsc.2018.2884928

27. Qiao, Y., Jiang, Q., Jiang, Z., Gu, L.: A multi-channel visualization method for malware classification based on deep learning. In: 18th IEEE International Conference on Trust, Security and Privacy in Computing and Communications/13th IEEE International Conference on Big Data Science and Engineering (TrustCom/BigDataSE), Rotorua, New Zealand, pp. 757–762 (2019)

28. Fu, J., Xue, J., Wang, Y., Liu, Z., Shan, C.: Malware visualization for fine-grained classification. IEEE Access **6**, 14510–14523 (2018). https://doi.org/10.1109/ACCESS.2018.2805301

29. Taheri, L., Kadir, A.F.A., Lashkari, A.H.: Extensible android malware detection and family classification using network-flows and API-calls. In: International Carnahan Conference on Security Technology (ICCST), Chennai, India, pp. 1–8 (2019). https://doi.org/10.1109/ccst.2019.8888430

30. Lashkari, A.H., Kadir, A.F., A., Taheri, L., Ghorbani, A.A.: Toward developing a systematic approach to generate benchmark android malware datasets and classification. In: International Carnahan Conference on Security Technology (ICCST), Montreal, QC, pp. 1–7 (2018). https://doi.org/10.1109/ccst.2018.8585560
31. Maldozer Karbab, E.B., Debbabi, M., Derhab, A., Mouheb, D.: MalDozer: automatic framework for android malware detection using deep learning. Digit. Invest. **24**, S48–S59 (2018)
32. Moonsamy, V., Rong, J., Liu, S.: Mining permission patterns for contrasting clean and malicious android applications. Future Gener. Comput. Syst. **36**(July), 122–132 (2014). https://doi.org/10.1016/j.future.2013.09.014

Vulnerability Database as a Service
for IoT

Mark Nerwich[1]([✉]), Praveen Gauravaram[2], Hye-young Paik[1][iD],
and Surya Nepal[3][iD]

[1] School of Computer Science and Engineering, University of New South Wales
(UNSW), Sydney, Australia
{m.nerwich,h.paik}@unsw.edu.au
[2] Tata Consultancy Services Limited (TCS), Brisbane, Australia
p.gauravaram@tcs.com
[3] CSIRO's Data61, Sydney, Australia
surya.nepal@data61.csiro.au

Abstract. In this paper we address the problem of lack of knowledge
management systems for Internet of Things (IoT)-specific vulnerabilities
and attacks. This data has been published in disparate sources including
news articles, blogs, white papers and social media but not in a centralised form. In addition, while comprehensive vulnerability databases
do exist, a significant portion of their listings may not apply to IoT
devices since these devices tend to run on unique software, hardware
and networking protocols. We present the design and implementation
of a community-driven, IoT-specific database which documents the vulnerabilities and attacks on IoT infrastructures. Our database supports
the integration with other vulnerability databases such as National Vulnerability Database (NVD) and provides a suite of data access APIs
for integration with other applications, such as Integrated Development
Environment (IDE) or security tools. The database can serve as a knowledge base for IoT application developers, and security researchers as well
as contribute to the cyber situational awareness in an enterprise and
improve general security awareness for the public over IoT security.

Keywords: IoT · Vulnerabilities · Database · Cyber attacks · Security
knowledge management

1 Introduction

Internet of Things (IoT) is a system of interconnected computing devices with an
ability to understand and comprehend, in any given situation, and take appropriate actions or decisions without any human interventions. As sensor technology
continues to become cheaper, more advanced and widely available, the trans-
formative influence of IoT-based applications is rapidly reaching many indus-
tries such as healthcare, manufacturing, transportation, utility, and energy &

L. Batina and G. Li (Eds.): ATIS 2020, CCIS 1338, pp. 95–107, 2020.
https://doi.org/10.1007/978-981-33-4706-9_7

resources. While IoT is becoming increasingly ubiquitous, its security vulnerabilities can be exploited to launch cyber attacks on the critical infrastructures. The prevalence of IoT vulnerabilities stems from the challenges faced by the IoT manufacturing industry such as unfamiliarity with the security practices, the use of third-party components, lack of regulation and resource-constrained cryptographic capabilities in the devices themselves. Hence it is important to build security knowledge management (SKM) databases that improve IoT security awareness among the stakeholders of IoT as well as address situational awareness of an enterprise once they are deployed for use.

We have noticed several gaps in the SKM of IoT devices. Firstly, we have not found any centralised disclosure of IoT exploits. IoT exploit data is often published in the form of disparate news articles, white papers, blogs and social media. Secondly, there is a lack of IoT-specific vulnerability disclosure. Although centralised vulnerability databases such as National Vulnerability Database (NVD) do exist, a significant portion of their listings may not apply to IoT devices since these devices tend to run on unique software, hardware and networking protocols, thus imposing challenges to present comprehensive security recommendations and listings [1,7]. The notion of IoT-specific vulnerabilities has not been represented in the literature to date and is the problem that we have undertaken to address in this paper.

In this paper, we present a community-based security and vulnerability report database for IoT devices to manage the knowledge of security incidents and related information. The database describes a set of attributes relating to a vulnerability or attack report with IoT context. The database is implemented as an API-focused serviceable software component that is easily accessible for the developers and security researchers and practitioners. The implementation of the database supports the integration with other vulnerability databases such as NVD and also community developed Common Weakness Enumeration (CWE). Integrating with CWE allows us to extract the details of vulnerability types that are associated with vulnerabilities listed in the NVD. The key feature of our NVD integration is matching a user's vulnerability or exploit report with data in the NVD, allowing us to build a high-quality database of IoT-specific data. Our database stores a unique data schema that adds real world information to the NVD's technical data, such as societal impact, organisations affected and the components responsible for the security risk. The APIs provide an opportunity for the database to be integrated with other applications such as IDE or digital forensic investigation tools.

The impact and applicability of our SKM study for IoT and IoT vulnerability database itself in the form of improved security awareness for diverse participants in the IoT ecosystem is outlined below:

- **Public**: SKM in the IoT space would be a useful tool to educate the general public, building awareness of security threats facing IoT devices and satisfying any curiosities that users may have regarding specific vulnerabilities, exploits/attacks[1] or trends.

---

[1] Throughout the paper, we use the term attacks and exploits interchangeably.

- **Vendors**: An SKM solution for IoT would enable vendors to understand the most likely vulnerabilities affecting their products and implement targeted defensive measures. By viewing reports of historical attacks, vendors are able to predict future attacks on their products and the impact of those attacks.
- **Consumers**: Consumers would like to understand the risks of using their IoT products in order to make more informed purchasing decisions. Detailed SKM of IoT products could act as a platform for these consumers to discover risks facing their products as well as the potential impact of those risks.
- **Security Researchers**: Security researchers could use an IoT-focused SKM solution to share their research outcomes as well as view the work of other researchers and members of the security community [5].
- **Businesses**: The IoT Vulnerability database could contribute to cyber situational awareness for the security staff of an enterprise over vulnerable IoT devices with information about firmware updates, patches and upgrading older versions of operating systems. In addition, by integrating with the components of executive level dashboards, the database can contribute to in-depth analysis on security events, allowing executives and board members to draw insightful conclusions and make logical inferences from the IoT specific data.
- **Data Miners**: SKM solutions that are well-curated offer the possibility of being subject to data mining techniques in order to reveal undiscovered patterns of vulnerabilities and exploits. For instance, [15] analyses vulnerability databases to detect the earliest point in time that a virus or worm emerges and to detect intrusion patterns. [14] uses data mining techniques on vulnerability databases to learn which vulnerability attributes frequently occur together. It is also acknowledged that additional novel or interesting patterns remain could be discovered with different data mining algorithms.

The rest of the paper is organised as follows. We discuss related work in Sect. 2. Sections 3 and 4 present the design and implementation of the vulnerability database for IoT, followed by Sect. 5 where we present the results of the evaluations. We conclude the paper in Sect. 6 with brief discussions and future directions for the work.

2 Related Work

Existing Security Databases and Related Standards: There are existing security related databases that are within the SKM area but may not refer directly to IoT security. Integrating our database with the IoT-specific data within these projects presents an opportunity to improve the depth and completeness of IoT-specific database proposed in our paper.

The *National Vulnerability Database (NVD)* is a collection of databases containing information on security checklist references, security related software flaws, misconfigurations, product names, and impact metrics [10]. It is run by the National Institute of Standards and Technology, which falls under the U.S. Department of Commerce. It is an extensive and comprehensive database that offers a small amount of analysis on each vulnerability, such as impact metrics and vulnerability types. It offers data feeds as a way for users to automate the processing of its entries. The vulnerabilities are not IoT specific, however many IoT devices run traditional software, making many of the NVD's entries relevant to IoT devices.

The *Common Vulnerability Scoring System (CVSS)* is an industry standard for assessing the severity of software vulnerabilities, assigning a score and a qualitative assessment based on several metrics [6]. *Common Vulnerabilities and Exposures (CVE)* and *Common Weakness Enumeration (CWE)* provide a list of common/standardised identifiers for cybersecurity vulnerabilities, maintained by the MITRE corporation and CVS/CVE communities [3]?. The CVE database provides a standarised identifiers to avoid the issue of different security databases referring to the same problem using different terms. The CWE database provides standardised categories for software weaknesses. The standard provides a unifying language of discourse, an ability to effectively compare and contrast weaknesses, and for users to easily understand the types of weaknesses they are dealing with [3]. These identifiers are utilised in many other security databases and tools including NVD.

Vulnerability Tools: There are are projects that concern the security of IoT devices but may not involve the disclosure of vulnerabilities or exploits. These works could provide an opportunity to be integrated with a vulnerability reporting database presented in our paper.

Shodan[2] is a search engine for devices connected to the internet. Many filters can be applied to the searches, allowing users to target specific types of IoT devices. It can be used in combination with other tools to assess network security, analyse global trends and discover vulnerabilities in devices. *Nessus* is a vulnerability scanner over many technologies including operating systems, IoT devices, databases and web applications. It was designed to scan large networks with thousands of devices and categorises vulnerabilities using the CVSS system[3]. Other vulnerability assessment tools include *Burp Suite, Qualys* and *Nexpose*, although these are not ideal for large-scale assessments [8].

Several papers have developed unique methods to scan networks to find vulnerabilities present in IoT devices. These could be used to automatically generate reports and populate a vulnerability database. Markowsky and Markowsky [8] developed methods targeting specific devices or specific exploits, while Su, Li, Wang, Yi and He target network transmission protocols to detect sensor vulnerabilities [12]. Another paper used public security analysis tools such as Shodan and Nessus to detect for vulnerabilities in medical devices [9].

Other Security Knowledge Management (SKM) Initiatives: In terms of other security knowledge management work share similar goals to our project,

---

[2] Shodan, https://www.shodan.io/.

[3] Tenable: Nessus, http://www.tenable.com/products/nessus.

the *Open Web Application Security Project (OWASP) Internet of Things Project* is designed to improve security outcomes by enabling developers, manufacturers, enterprises and consumers to make better security decisions. It provides a list of the top ten things to avoid when building, deploying or managing IoT systems, as well as detailed lists of IoT attack surface areas, vulnerabilities and testing guides [13]. [5] proposed a conceptual system architecture and process design to integrate various existing security database sources. [16] presented an integrated vulnerability database that included CVE, NVD and IBM X-Force[4] as their main sources. However, these efforts target generic cyber security areas, not specialised in IoT. It is worth noting that UK government's *Code of Practice for Consumer IoT Security* provides specific guidance for IoT manufacturers to achieve a "secure by design" approach. Key guidelines include stating that IoT devices must have unique passwords, vulnerability disclosure policies must be in place and devices should be receptive to software updates [2].

3   Solution Design and Requirements

In this section, we describe the design of the database and user requirements for implementing the system.

3.1   IoT Vulnerability/Attack Report Schema

We studied existing security databases to consider what we need to capture in our database. To accommodate IoT related features as much as possible, we also examined many online articles on reporting IoT attacks. Our database has 17 attributes, including: source, category, date, description, device type, vulnerability/attack source, related parties, severity, impact, security property compromised, CVE number, patch information, etc. Each entry may not have values for all attributes, but the intention of our design is that these attributes can be filled in by the community members over time as the information become available. We list some of the main attributes and their meaning below. The category of each report is either 'vulnerability' or 'attack' and some attributes are only relevant to one category.

3.2   User Contribution Workflow

As reflected in the schema, there are two types of reporting that our database captures: security attacks, and vulnerabilities. It is noted that not all known vulnerabilities end up being exploited by the attackers, so being able to collect both types of information in a knowledge base like ours could help analyse possible links between the two types of information.

We build a web application as the "front-end" of the database. The web application provides a user interface for collecting reports from the users. It also

---

[4] IBM X-force Exchange, http://www.exchange.xforce.ibmcloud.com.

displays vulnerability and attack reports with search functionality. The Web application collects these reports differently depending on its type as illustrated in Fig. 1 (Table 1):

Table 1. Example attributes of a vulnerability report in our database.

Name	Data	Applies to
Description	A textual description of the vulnerability or attack	Vulnerabilities and attacks
Device type	A description on the type of IoT device(s) affected	Vulnerabilities and attacks
Vulnerability source	The technical component(s) responsible for the vulnerability	Vulnerabilities only
Related parties	Any entity (commercial or non-commercial) involved in, or impacted by the vulnerability or attack	Vulnerabilities and attacks
Impact	Description of impact, split into three areas: industry, social & business	Attacks only
Security properties compromised	A list of security properties compromised by the vulnerability or attack, such as confidentiality, availability, integrity or non-repudiation	Vulnerabilities and attacks

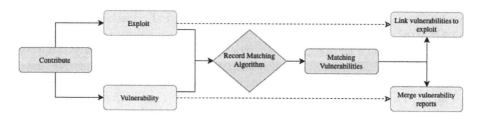

Fig. 1. User Contribution Workflow - creating entries to the database

1. *Attacks.* Attack reports are entered by users and submitted to the database. In this case, the application will attempt to match the report with known vulnerabilities that (from NVD) may have been used in the attack. The user has the option to link their attack report with these vulnerabilities, in which case the vulnerability reports will be submitted to the database alongside the attack report.
2. *Vulnerabilities.* Vulnerability reports are entered by users and submitted to the database. In this case, the application will attempt to match the report with the same vulnerability stored in a comprehensive, third party database such as the NVD. The user has the option to merge their report with the report from the NVD.

3.3   Interfaces - Users and Data Access APIs

The user interface allows users to interact with the vulnerability database in a graphically-friendly manner. An example of the interface is shown in Fig. 2. Some of the main user stories we defined and implemented are:

- *I want to view the latest vulnerabilities and attacks on IoT devices, so that I can stay up to date on the state of IoT cyber security,*
- *I want to view vulnerabilities and attacks facing a specific IoT device, so I know the most likely cyber security issues facing a device that I may use,*
- *I want to search for a vulnerability or an attack for some details,*
- *I want to upload a vulnerability or attack report to the database, so that I can share my work and contribute to improving IoT security,*
- *I want to merge my vulnerability report with a vulnerability report from a comprehensive vulnerability database if they refer to the same vulnerability, so that my vulnerability report can have improved detail, coverage and reputability,*
- *I want to link my attack report with one or more vulnerability reports that may have been used to achieve the exploitation.*

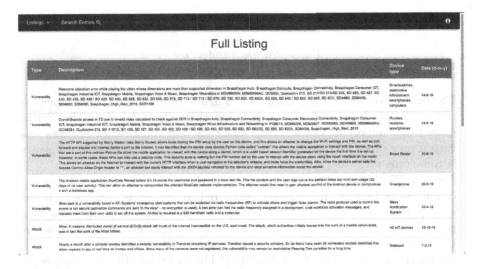

Fig. 2. Full listing of report entries

Besides the user interface, we also developed the application programming interface (API) allow other software systems to dynamically interact with the database. These APIs are designed to make integration with other applications, such as IDE, possible. Some of the representative API methods are listed below.

- ***GET/all_entries***: *returns an array of objects containing all vulnerability and attack information.*
- ***GET/search_entries***: *returns an array of all objects that contain values that are equal to the keys specified in the request object.*

- **_GET/keyword_search_**: _returns an array of all objects that contain values that are equal to the keys specified in the request object._
- **_POST/match_entry_**: _returns an array of matching NVD vulnerabilities_
- **_POST/add_entry_**: _submits an entry to the database._

4   Implementation

The implemented architecture of the database and Web application has the following key components (Fig. 3):

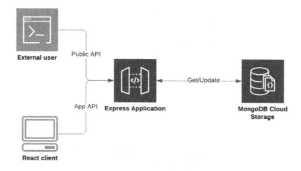

Fig. 3. System architecture

- **Express** server framework. Express is a lightweight, flexible API framework written in **Node.js**, which is a language that allows full-stack JavaScript developing, improving development efficiency and consistency. Express was chosen over other frameworks because its lightweight and basic functionality is consistent with the programming requirements of this project.
- **MongoDB Atlas** database. This is a platform that provides a collection of databases that are hosted and monitored in the cloud. MongoDB is the most popular NoSQL, document-storage database and is both free and open source. Its NoSQL design is advantageous as it accommodates for changing data models.
- **React** client library. React is a JavaScript library for building user interfaces. It is developed by Facebook and is extremely popular due to its simplicity and lack of boilerplate.

4.1   Data Management

The back-end repository implements several functional modules to maintain the records as duplicate free as possible. They play an important role during the following processes:

Importing NVD data feeds: Converting a vulnerability report supplied by a data feed from the NVD [11] to a vulnerability report that is suitable for our database. This process requires the following mapping tasks to extract data from the NVD feeds to our own vulnerability database schema:

- The database extracts relevant information from the feed, such as date, description, severity, vendors and links.
- The database extracts vulnerability type by its Common Weakness Enumeration (CWE) code and performs a search inside the CWE database to include the name and description for that particular vulnerability type.

Similarity Match: Matching a user's entry with existing (converted) NVD entries. This process works by firstly extracting the keywords from the user's entry by removing stop words, using a third-party library called keyword-extractor [4]. Then, the chosen keywords are used to search through all converted NVD entries. The top 5 matches are displayed to the user. As part of future work, it would be interesting to use artificial intelligence to improve on this algorithm that matches users' reports to NVD vulnerabilities.

4.2   Handling User Input

In order for the database to be successful in achieving its aims, the data must be of sufficiently high quality and quantity. However, the database relies heavily on participation from the security community to supply data for the database. Hence we must take steps to automatically improve these outcomes.

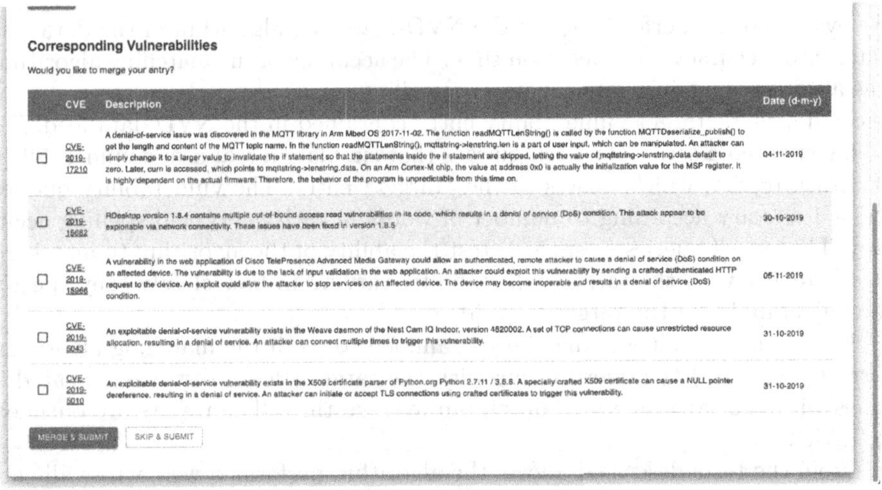

Fig. 4. Merge vulnerability with NVD vulnerabilities

Quality. In this project, we assume that vulnerability reports stored in comprehensive and standardised vulnerability databases such as the NVD are likely to be of higher quality than those entered by a user. To this end, when a user enters a vulnerability report, the application automatically matches it to corresponding NVD entries, giving the option to capture all extra information from this NVD entry. See Fig. 4 for a screenshot of this feature.

Quantity. When a user enters an attack report, the application automatically matches it to corresponding NVD entries, which refer to vulnerabilities that may have been used in the attack. All vulnerabilities that the user chooses to incorporate are imported into the database alongside the user-entered report. This has the potential to vastly increase the number of IoT-specific entries in the database.

4.3   Collating IoT-Specific Vulnerabilities

We define IoT-specific vulnerabilities to be software or hardware vulnerabilities present in IoT devices or in the infrastructures that support them. We collect these vulnerabilities by targeting the vulnerabilities that have been exploited during an attack on an IoT device ecosystem. For example, a user may report an attack on a set of IoT devices. With our NVD-integration feature, we attempt to search for the vulnerabilities that were exploited in this attack. Matching vulnerabilities are then incorporated into our database, ensuring the collation of IoT-specific vulnerabilities. This will complement the vulnerability reports entered by the users.

5   Performance and Evaluation

We evaluated the performance of the NVD-matching algorithm in the database in terms of accuracy and execution time. The accuracy of the matching algorithm was also tested against its resilience to spelling errors. To perform the tests, we selected a single target vulnerability entry contained in the NVD data feed. We then generated a series of search queries that simulate a real user's vulnerability or attack report, which relates to the "target" entry. The vulnerability queries (tests 1–4) vary according to number of words in each query and spelling accuracy. The attack queries (tests 5–6) test the ability of the algorithm to match an attack report with the target vulnerability, varying in how closely they specify the vulnerability in the target (Fig. 5).

Each search result was manually examined to see if the matching algorithm correctly matched the query terms with the targets. Each test was repeated 3 times with the same query to obtain an average time. The results are outlined in Table 2.

From the tests described above, the algorithm performed well across all categories. The target match was present in all instances of the test and displayed first, as the strongest match. Although the response time was not insignificant, at 807 ms minimum, it showed very small increases with size of input and match difficulty, demonstrating strong scalability.

```
{
    "category": "Attack",
    "date": "8/12/18",
    "description": "attack on a smart fridge using a flaw in the CoAP protocol",
    "deviceType": "smart fridge",
    "vulnerabilitySource": "CoAP",
    "vulnerabilityType": "integer overflow",
    "relatedParties": ""
}
```

Fig. 5. Test query 5 - related attack (specific)

Table 2. Evaluation of matching algorithm performance. The position of the match ranges from 0–4, 0 being the first, 4 being the last.

	Description	Query size (bytes)	Avg. time (ms)	Target match present	Position of the match
1	Small input	241	816	Yes	0
2	Medium input	519	833	Yes	0
3	Large input	709	814	Yes	0
4	Spelling mistakes (small input)	246	807	Yes	0
5	Related attack (specific)	272	829	Yes	0
6	Related attack (unspecific)	256	857	Yes	0

6   Conclusions

This paper presents a Proof of Concept system of IoT vulnerability and exploit database. The system supports the integration with NVD and CWE and provides a suite of data access APIs for integration with other applications. Our paper attempts to answer the questions: (i) What information would users want to see?, (ii) How can we get a complete set of that information? by developing a solution to extract relevant data, utilising integrations with NVD and CWE, storing it in our database and publishing to users via a website and APIs.

With regards to IoT attacks, users want to see both technical and non-technical details of attacks on IoT devices. Our work assumes manual entry of content to the database. The prevalence of security researchers who go out of their way to contact external parties upon discovering vulnerabilities gives us a reasonable confidence that users will not be averse to entering IoT attack records into our database. However, as a future direction, it would be interesting to automate the whole discovery and ingestion process.

With regards to IoT vulnerabilities, we assumed that users want to see IoT-specific vulnerability information. This led to the question of what defines an IoT-specific vulnerability? Whilst there are some IoT-exclusive networking protocols (e.g., MQTT and CoAP), most IoT applications run conventional software either on the device itself or in the cloud, defeating the notion of an IoT-specific vulnerability. Furthermore, including all vulnerabilities that could potentially impact IoT devices would lead to a duplication of NVD. Hence, a valuable future research direction would be to investigate what subset of all vulnerabilities apply most specifically to IoT devices and build the database accordingly.

In addition, it is important to undertake a rigorous formal security model and proofs of security for the presented solution and its improvements and validate against the experimental analysis.

Acknowledgement. The work has been supported by the Cyber Security Research Centre Limited whose activities are partially funded by the Australian Government's Cooperative Research Centres Programme. We also would like to thank Tata Consultancy Services Limited (TCS) and Data61, the industry partners of the program.

References

1. Alladi, T., Chamola, V., Sikdar, B., Choo, K.R.: Consumer IoT: security vulnerability case studies and solutions. IEEE Consum. Electron. Mag. **9**(2), 17–25 (2020)
2. Blythe, J., Johnson, S.: The consumer security index for IoT: a protocol for developing an index to improve consumer decision making and to incentivize greater security provision in IoT devices. IET Conference Proceedings, pp. 4–7, January 2018
3. Common Weakness Enumeration: About CWE (2019). http://cwe.mitre.org/about/index.html. Accessed 16 Aug 2019
4. Delorenzo, M.: Keyword Extractor. https://github.com/michaeldelorenzo/keyword-extractor. Accessed 22 Jul 2020
5. Fedorchenko, A., Kotenko, I., Chechulin, A.: Integrated repository of security information for network security evaluation. J. Wirel. Mob. Netw. Ubiquitous Comput. Dependable Appl. **6**, 41–57 (2015)
6. FIRST: Common Vulnerability Scoring System SIG. http://cwe.mitre.org/about/index.html. Accessed July 2020
7. Jing, Q., Vasilakos, A.V., Wan, J., Lu, J., Qiu, D.: Security of the internet of things: perspectives and challenges. Wireless Netw. **20**(8), 2481–2501 (2014). https://doi.org/10.1007/s11276-014-0761-7
8. Markowsky, L., Markowsky, G.: Scanning for vulnerable devices in the Internet of Things. In: IEEE 8th International Conference on Intelligent Data Acquisition and Advanced Computing Systems: Technology and Applications (IDAACS), pp. 463–467 (2015)
9. McMahon, E., Williams, R., El, M., Samtani, S., Patton, M., Chen, H.: Assessing medical device vulnerabilities on the internet of things. In: IEEE International Conference on Intelligence and Security Informatics (ISI), pp. 176–178 (2017)
10. National Vulnerability Database: General information. https://nvd.nist.gov/general. Accessed Oct 2020
11. National Vulnerability Database: NVD Data Feeds. https://nvd.nist.gov/vuln/data-feeds. Accessed 16 Aug 2019

12. Su, Y., Li, X., Wang, S., Yi, J., He, H.: Vulnerability scanning system used in the internet of things for intelligent devices. In: DEStech Transactions on Computer Science and Engineering cimns (2017)

13. Shoel, H., Jaatun, M.G., Boyd, C.: OWASP top 10 - do startups care? In: 2018 International Conference on Cyber Security and Protection of Digital Services (Cyber Security), pp. 1–8 (2018)

14. Tierney, S.: Knowledge discovery in cyber vulnerability databases. Master's thesis, Computing and Software Systems, University of Washington (2005)

15. Yamanishi, J., Maruyama, Y.: Data mining for security. NEC J. Adv. Technol. **2**(1), 63–69 (2005)

16. Yun-hua, G., Pei, L.: Design and research on vulnerability database. In: 3rd International Conference on Information and Computing, pp. 209–212 (2010)

Linear and Partly-Pseudo-Linear Cryptanalysis of Reduced-Round SPARX Cipher

Sarah Alzakari[✉] and Poorvi Vora

The George Washington University, Washington DC 20052, USA
salzakari@gwu.edu

Abstract. We propose a new cryptanalytic technique and key recovery attack for the SPARX cipher, *Partly-Pseudo-Linear Cryptanalysis*, a meet-in-the-middle attack combining linear and pseudo-linear approximations. We observe improvements over the linear hull attacks in the literature for SPARX 128/128 and 128/256. Additionally, we generate another attack for comparison purposes, using the Cho-Pieprzyk property for a fully-linear approximation and a corresponding key recovery attack. We observe improvements on the data complexity, bias, and number of recovered key bits, over all variants of SPARX, when compared to the use of only the Cho-Pieprzyk approximation.

Keywords: SPARX · Pseudo-Linear cryptanalysis · Linear cryptanalysis · Partly-Pseudo-Linear cryptanalysis

1 Introduction

SPARX is a lightweight cipher, intended for use in cryptographic applications on devices with power constraints. It is designed to have low memory, computational capacity and power requirements. It is an instance of an ARX block cipher—which rely on Addition-Rotation-XOR operations performed a number of times, and provide a common approach to lightweight cipher design. The use of addition makes ARX ciphers more robust to traditional linear cryptanalysis, and new approaches to cryptanalysis are necessary to analyze ARX ciphers. This paper presents a new approximation and corresponding key recovery attack, the *Partly-Pseudo-Linear Attack* on the SPARX family.

1.1 Our Contributions

We propose the Partly-Pseudo-Linear Attack which combines pseudo-linear approximation with a linear approximation of addition modulo 2^n using Cho and Pieprzyk's property of modular addition [3,4]. We are able to demonstrate an improvement over linear hull attacks on SPARX in the literature. In particular, our contributions are as follows:

© Springer Nature Singapore Pte Ltd. 2020
L. Batina and G. Li (Eds.): ATIS 2020, CCIS 1338, pp. 108–121, 2020.
https://doi.org/10.1007/978-981-33-4706-9_8

1. For the purposes of comparison with our main contribution, the Partly-Pseudo-Linear Attack, we apply fully linear cryptanalysis on the SPARX family using the Cho-Pieprzyk property to obtain a linear approximation and a corresponding key recovery attack. We use the approach presented by Ashur and Bodden for SPECK [1].
2. We propose the Partly-Pseudo-Linear Attack on SPARX: a combination of a pseudo-linear approximation for a few rounds and a linear approximation for the rest. We describe and analyze the corresponding key recovery attacks and perform the following comparisons:
   - We are not aware of linear key recovery attacks for SPARX in the literature. We compare our key recovery attacks to recent contributions of linear trails on SPARX using linear hulls, by extending the linear trails in a natural way to include as many decryption rounds as allowed by computational complexity considerations. Our results are better for the larger variants.
   - We observe improvements across all variants due to our partly-pseudo-linear approximation when compared to the use of only the Cho-Pieprzyk approximation.

1.2   Comparison with Closest Other Work

The SPARX cipher is a very recent design, proposed in 2016 [5,8]. The literature on SPARX is hence limited. Most of the literature is focused on differential and linear (hull) cryptanalysis. The closest work is a 2020 report on linear hull cryptanalysis [7]. Huang and Wang present an automatic algorithm to search for the optimal linear (hull) characteristics on ARX ciphers using Wallen's algorithm for modular addition [12]. Table 1 summarizes the comparison between our contributions and [7].

Table 1. The results of this work and the linear hull cryptanalysis on SPARX cipher.

N	Ref.	Type	Number of rounds	Guessed key Bit/K	Bias	Data	Time
64	[7]	Linear Hull	11	LT	2^{-28}	N/A	N/A
	[7]	Linear Hull	10	LT	2^{-22}	N/A	N/A
	This work	LC	9	60/128	2^{-23}	2^{46}	2^{106}
	This work	PPLC	9	93/128	$2^{-15.84}$	2^{32}	2^{125}
128	[7]	Linear Hull	10	LT	2^{-23}	N/A	N/A
	[7]	Linear Hull	9	LT	2^{-18}	N/A	N/A
	This work	LC	9	44/128	2^{-19}	2^{38}	2^{82}
	This work	LC	10	140/256	2^{-19}	2^{38}	2^{178}
	This work	PPLC	9	98/128	$2^{-13.73}$	2^{28}	2^{126}
	This work	PPLC	11	195/256	$2^{-20.42}$	2^{42}	2^{237}

* N is the block size and K is the key size.
* LT refers to a Linear Trail used as a distinguisher and NA refers to Not Available.
* PPLC refers to the Partly-Pseudo-Linear Cryptanalysis and LC refers to the Linear Cryptanalysis

Huang and Wang do not describe key recovery, but their work could possibly be extended to key recovery attacks by appending rounds of decryption.

- SPARX 64/128: The linear approximation of [7] is already deeper than our key recovery attack.
- SPARX 128/128: The linear approximation of [7] cannot be used as a key recovery attack since the round has 128 key bits.
- SPARX 128/256: [7] can add one more round to recover 128 key bits. Thus the number of rounds they would be able to attack would be the same as ours, but our attack provides more recovered key bits and has lower data complexity.

1.3   Organization

This paper is organized as follows. In Sect. 2, we present a brief description of the SPARX cipher and the notation used in this paper. In Sect. 3 we review linear cryptanalysis and pseudo-linear cryptanalysis. In Sect. 4, we present our first contribution by applying the linear cryptanalysis on SPARX family. In Sect. 5, we present our proposed Partly-Pseudo-Linear attack on the SPARX cipher. We conclude in Sect. 6.

2   Preliminaries

This section presents our notation and briefly describes the SPARX cipher.

2.1   Notation

The following describes notation used in this paper.

- $\boxplus_n$: Addition modulo 2^n
- $\boxminus_n$: Subtraction modulo 2^n
- $PL(CL)$: Left word of the Plaintext (Ciphertext)
- $PR(CR)$: Right word of the Plaintext (Ciphertext)
- xl^{j-1}: Left half of input to the jth round
- xr^{j-1}: Right half of input to the jth round
- $xl_t^j(i, i+w)$: window t with size w of the Left word x, where the MSB is at i and the LSB is at $i + w - 1$, for $0 \le i < \frac{n}{2}$ and $1 \le w \le \frac{n}{2}$
- $xr_t^j(i, i+w)$: window t with size w of the Right word x, where the MSB is at i and the LSB is at $i + w - 1$, for $0 \le i < \frac{n}{2}$ and $1 \le w \le \frac{n}{2}$

2.2   The SPARX Cipher

In 2016, Dinu et al. proposed the SPARX family of ARX block ciphers [5,8]. The instance of the SPARX family with block size n and key size k is denoted SPARX n/k. The only operations needed to implement an instance of SPARX are:

- Addition modulo 2^{16}, denoted $\boxplus$
- 16-bit Rotation: right rotation by i, denoted $\ggg i$ and left rotation by i, denoted $i \lll$
- 16-bit exclusive-or (XOR), denoted $\oplus$

The non-linearity in SPARX is provided by *Speckey*; a 32-bit block cipher identical to Speck 32 except for its key injection (Speckey is denoted by A in Fig. 1 and Fig. 2). The round function consists of exclusive-or with the key, followed by Speckey. In SPARX 64/128, a linear permutation (denoted by $\mathcal{L}$ in Fig. 1) follows three rounds. In SPARX 128/128 and SPARX 128/256, the linear permutation (denoted by $\mathcal{L}'$ in Fig. 2) follows four rounds (Table 2).

Table 2. The SPARX cipher family.

Block Size, n	No. words, $n/32$	Key size	Steps	No. rounds/step
64	2	128	8	3
128	4	128	8	4
	4	256	10	4

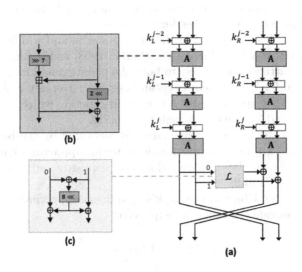

Fig. 1. SPARX 64/128. (a) Three rounds function, (b) Speckey and (c) Linear permutation.

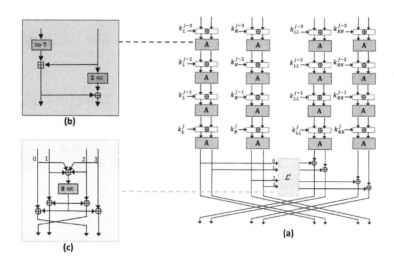

Fig. 2. SPARX 128/128 and SPARX 128/256. (a) Four rounds function, (b) Speckey and (c) Linear permutation.

3 Related Work

In this section, We review linear cryptanalysis and pseudo-linear cryptanalysis, as we will use these two approaches for our attack.

Linear cryptanalysis [9] is one of the most powerful and widely used attacks on block ciphers. It was introduced by Matsui in 1998, and is a known plaintext attack where the attacker has access to both the plaintext and its encrypted version ciphertext [6,9]. Using linear cryptanalysis, an adversary is able to find a linear expression that approximates a non-linear function which connects plaintext, ciphertext, and key bits with high probability.

The quality of the linear approximation is measured by the bias ϵ which is defined as $\epsilon = |p - \frac{1}{2}|$; a higher bias implies a better approximation and a more efficient attack. The number of required known plaintexts and ciphertexts (data complexity) is $O(\epsilon^{-2})$ [6,9].

Our work relies on Cho and Pieprzyk's [3,4] linear approximation of modular addition. They provide the following expression

$$P[\lambda.(a \boxplus b) = \lambda.(a \oplus b)] = \frac{3}{4} \tag{1}$$

where λ is a mask identifying the consecutive bits we are interested in. Importantly, one may use this approximation over multiple rounds in an ARX cipher only so long as any masks encountered in the round function entering into the modular addition do not containing non-consecutive bits.

McKay and Vora [10,11] present pseudo-linear cryptanalysis which aims to overcome the limitations of traditional linear cryptanalysis by approximating addition modulo 2^n with addition modulo 2^w where, $0 < w \leq n$. In other words, the pseudo-linear approximations use addition modulo 2^w and exclusive-or over w-bit strings of contiguous bits (or windows) instead of using the whole n-bit strings.

This approximation is in error only when the carry into the last bit of the window is one. If the value of the carry is equally likely to be zero or one, the approximation is correct with probability slightly greater than a half, which is much larger than the probability of a random guess which is $\frac{1}{2^w}$. The approximation involves the use of some key bits in non-linear operations, but enables attacks more efficient than the brute force attack because it reduces the number of key bits from those required by the cipher.

The only linear cryptanalysis available to date on SPARX is that of Huang and Wang [7], described in Sect. 1.2.

4   Linear Cryptanalysis on the SPARX Family

The purpose of this contribution is to explore the improvement of our proposed *Partly-Pseudo-Linear Cryptanalysis* on a fully-linear attack. In particular, we study the effect of replacing some rounds of linear cryptanalysis with pseudo-linear cryptanalysis. For this reason, we first study the fully-linear attack.

In this section, we analyze the ARX lightweight block cipher family, SPARX, to determine its resistance to the Cho-Pieprzyk approximation of modular addition. In the next section, Sect. 5, we demonstrate the improvement in this cryptanalysis if a couple of rounds of linear approximations are replaced with pseudo-linear approximations.

For linear cryptanalysis, we take the approach of Ashur and Bodden's cryptanalysis of the SPECK family [1]. We search for the best approximation using Cho-Pieprzyk's property. The left word is divided into two blocks, left and right block. We start by fixing one mask (left block) λ_x^L with a pair of consecutive bits $(0x3, 0x6, ...)$ and zeroing the other mask (right block) λ_y^L. For the right word, we zero both left and right block masks. We check how the masks evolve both in the forward and backward direction taking into consideration the linear permutation after every three (or four, for the larger variants) rounds.

First we present the linear approximation and the corresponding key recovery attack on SPARX 64/128 then on SPARX 128/128 and SPARX 128/256.

The longest linear trail we were able to find for SPARX 64/128 covers 7 rounds (we are able to go to 8 rounds for the right word). Table 9 shows how the mask changes: $\lambda_{x^i}^L$ represents the input mask of the left block of the left word of SPARX and $\lambda_{y^i}^L$ represents the input mask of the right block of the left word of SPARX. Similarly, $\lambda_{x^i}^R$ and $\lambda_{y^i}^R$ are input masks for the left and right blocks of the right word. We observe that the first linear permutation does not change anything since the left word is masked by zero.

With $\lambda = \text{0x000c000000000000}$ ($\lambda^L = \text{0x000c0000}$ $\lambda^R = \text{0x00000000}$), we can go 5 rounds in the backward direction and 2 rounds in the forward direction. For the right word of SPARX 64/128, the mask can go one more round deeper.

To implement a key recovery attack over nine rounds, we decrypt two more rounds for the left word, trying all possibilities for the active key bits in our linear approximation. For the right word, we need to decrypt a single round by trying all possibilities for the key bits that lead to the mask of the eighth round of the right word (see Fig. 3). Table 9 in the Appendix summarizes the progression of the mask for the linear key recovery attack on SPARX 64/128.

As for SPARX 64/128, we begin by searching for the best Cho-Pieprzyk approximation for SPARX 128/128 and 128/256. With

$$\lambda = \texttt{0x000c000000000000000000000000000000}$$

we can approximate 8 rounds, 4 in each direction. To implement a key recovery attack, we decrypt one more round by trying all possibilities for the key bits that lead to the mask of the eighth rounds for SPARX 128/128 and decrypt two rounds for SPARX 128/256. Table 3 summarizes the results of linear key recovery with Cho-Pieprzyk approximations on the SPARX family.

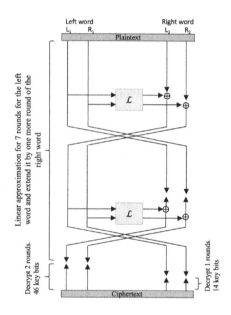

Fig. 3. Key recovery attack on SPARX 64/128 - 9 rounds

5   Partly-Pseudo-Linear Cryptanalysis on the SPARX Family

In this section, we present a new attack for the ARX block cipher which we term the *Partly-Pseudo-Linear Attack*.

Table 3. Linear key recovery attack on SPARX family

N/K	No. rounds of linear trail	No. rounds key recovery	Guessed bits	Bias	Data complexity	Time complexity
64/128	8	9	60	2^{-23}	2^{46}	2^{106}
128/128	8	9	44	2^{-19}	2^{38}	2^{82}
128/256	8	10	140	2^{-19}	2^{38}	2^{178}

* N is the block size and K is the key size.

Definition 1. *Partly-Pseudo-Linear Attack is a meet-in-the-middle combination of pseudo-linear and linear attacks.*

We show that linear cryptanalysis relying on Cho-Pieprzyk approximations of modular addition is improved by replacing some rounds of linear approximation with pseudo-linear approximations. Using the approach of Bodden and Ashur [1,2], we find the longest linear trails to approximate a window of two consecutive bits in each direction (forward and backward). Of these, we choose the trail(s) that would combine with a lower-error pseudo-linear attack.

The bias of the resulting Partly-Pseudo-Linear approximation hence consists of two parts. The first part is the bias of the xor of the bits of the window when the window is computed using the pseudo-linear approximation; this is determined experimentally. The second part is the bias for the linear approximation computed using traditional linear approaches. The combination of these two biases using the piling up lemma allows us to determine the number of plaintext and ciphertext pairs that we should use in our experiments. We illustrate and analyze the efficiency of our Partly-Pseudo-Linear cryptanalysis attack on all variants of the SPARX family.

5.1   The Partly-Pseudo-Linear Attack on Sparx 64/128

We first describe the Partly-Pseudo-Linear attack obtained by approximating nine rounds of SPARX 64/128. In the 9-round attack, we encrypt one round using all possibilities of the key bits that leads to our linear approximation (32 key bits of the right word). Then we approximate five rounds in the forward direction using linear approximation and three rounds in the backward direction using pseudo-linear approximation.

For the pseudo-linear approximation, the window size is two, $w = 2$, and 61 key bits are required for the approximation. In the last round the addition operation (subtraction) is before the key round injection; thus, it can be performed exactly for the full word without any need for an approximation.

For the linear approximation, we start the mask with $\lambda_x^L = \texttt{0x0000}$ and $\lambda_y^L = \texttt{0x0000}$ for the left word and $\lambda_x^R = \texttt{0x07f8}$ and $\lambda_y^R = \texttt{0xdf4}$ for the right word. Table 4 shows how the mask changes through the five rounds and the approximation for the Partly-Pseudo-Linear attack for 9 rounds is available in the appendix (see Table 8).

Table 4. Linear trail of SPARX 64/128 for 6 rounds

Round	Cost	Left Word				Right Word			
		$\lambda^L_{x^i}$	$\lambda^L_{y^i}$	$\lambda^L_{x^{i+1}}$	$\lambda^L_{y^{i+1}}$	$\lambda^R_{x^i}$	$\lambda^R_{y^i}$	$\lambda^R_{x^{i+1}}$	$\lambda^R_{y^{i+1}}$
1	0	0x0000	0x0000	0x0000	0x0000	Encrypt trying all key possibilities			
2	4	0x0000	0x0000	0x0000	0x0000	0x07f8	0xfdf4	0xc7e3	0x37ec
3	5	0x0000	0x0000	0x0000	0x0000	0xc7e3	0x37ec	0x0600	0xc18f
Linear permutation									
4	1	0x0600	0xc18f	0x0603	0x060f	0x0000	0x0000	0x0000	0x0000
5	2	0x0603	0x060f	0x0600	0x000c	0x0000	0x0000	0x0000	0x0000
6	1	0x0600	0x000c	0x000c	0x0000	0x0000	0x0000	0x0000	0x0000
Linear permutation									
		0x0c0c	0x0c00			0x000c	0x0000		

5.2 The Partly-Pseudo-Linear Attack on Sparx 128/128 and Sparx 128/256

The Partly-Pseudo-Linear attack on SPARX 128/128 is obtained by approximating 9 rounds: 4 in the forward direction using pseudo-linear approximation, 4 in the backward direction using linear approximation and one decryption round using all possibilities of the key bits that lead to our linear approximation (44 key bits of the first, second, and third words). For the pseudo-linear approximation, the window size is two, $w = 2$, and 54 key bits are required for the approximation. Table 5 shows how the mask for the linear approximation changes through the four rounds.

The Partly-Pseudo-Linear attack on SPARX 128/256 is obtained by approximating 11 rounds: two encryption rounds using all possibilities of the key bits leading to our linear approximation (64 key bits of the third word), 6 rounds in the forward direction using linear approximation and three rounds in the backward direction using pseudo-linear approximation. For the pseudo-linear approximation, the window size is two, $w = 2$, and 124 key bits are required for the approximation. In the last round the addition operation (subtraction) is before the key round injection; thus, it can be performed exactly for the full word without any need for an approximation. Table 6 shows how the mask for the linear approximation changes through the 6 rounds. Figure 4 describes the Partly-Pseudo-Linear attack on SPARX 128/128 and SPARX 128/256 and Table 7 summarizes the characteristics of the Partly-Pseudo-Linear attack on SPARX family.

Table 5. Linear trail of SPARX 128/128 for 9-round Partly-Pseudo-Linear approximation

Round	Cost	First word $\lambda_{x^i}^{L1}$	$\lambda_{y^i}^{R1}$	Second word $\lambda_{x^i}^{L2}$	$\lambda_{y^i}^{R2}$	Third word λ_{x}^{L3}	$\lambda_{y^i}^{R3}$	Fourth word $\lambda_{x^i}^{L4}$	$\lambda_{y^i}^{R4}$
5	1	0x000c	0x0000	0x0000	0x0000	0x0000	0x0000	0x0000	0x0000
		0x7800	0x6000	0x0000	0x0000	0x0000	0x0000	0x0000	0x0000
6	2	0x7800	0x6000	0x0000	0x0000	0x0000	0x0000	0x0000	0x0000
		0x8331	0x83c1	0x0000	0x0000	0x0000	0x0000	0x0000	0x0000
7	3	0x8331	0x83c1	0x0000	0x0000	0x0000	0x0000	0x0000	0x0000
		0xe019	0x831f	0x0000	0x0000	0x0000	0x0000	0x0000	0x0000
8	3	0xe019	0x831f	0x0000	0x0000	0x0000	0x0000	0x0000	0x0000
		0xf0be	0xc37e	0x0000	0x0000	0x0000	0x0000	0x0000	0x0000
Linear permutation									
		0x308d	0xc033	0xc033	0x034d	0xf0be	0xc37e	0x0000	0x0000

Table 6. Linear trail of SPARX 128/256 for 11-round Partly-Pseudo-Linear approximation

Round	Cost	First word $\lambda_{x^i}^{L1}$	$\lambda_{y^i}^{R1}$	Second word $\lambda_{x^i}^{L2}$	$\lambda_{y^i}^{R2}$	Third word λ_{x}^{L3}	$\lambda_{y^i}^{R3}$	Fourth word $\lambda_{x^i}^{L4}$	$\lambda_{y^i}^{R4}$
1	0	0x0000	0x0000	0x0000	0x0000	Try all 32 key bits		0x0000	0x0000
		0x0000	0x0000	0x0000	0x0000			0x0000	0x0000
2	0	0x0000	0x0000	0x0000	0x0000	Try all 32 key bits		0x0000	0x0000
		0x0000	0x0000	0x0000	0x0000			0x0000	0x0000
3	4	0x0000	0x0000	0x0000	0x0000	0x07f8	0xfdf4	0x0000	0x0000
		0x0000	0x0000	0x0000	0x0000	0xc7e3	0x37ec	0x0000	0x0000
4	5	0x0000	0x0000	0x0000	0x0000	0xc7e3	0x37ec	0x0000	0x0000
		0x0000	0x0000	0x0000	0x0000	0x0600	0xc18f	0x0000	0x0000
Linear permutation									
5	1	0x0600	0xc18f	0x0000	0x0000	0x0000	0x0000	0x0000	0x0000
		0x0603	0x060f	0x0000	0x0000	0x0000	0x0000	0x0000	0x0000
6	2	0x0603	0x060f	0x0000	0x0000	0x0000	0x0000	0x0000	0x0000
		0x0600	0x000c	0x0000	0x0000	0x0000	0x0000	0x0000	0x0000
7	1	0x0600	0x000c	0x0000	0x0000	0x0000	0x0000	0x0000	0x0000
		0x000c	0x0000	0x0000	0x0000	0x0000	0x0000	0x0000	0x0000
8	1	0x000c	0x0000	0x0000	0x0000	0x0000	0x0000	0x0000	0x0000
		0x7800	0x6000	0x0000	0x0000	0x0000	0x0000	0x0000	0x0000
Linear permutation									
		0x7818	0x0018	0x0018	0x6018	0x7800	0x6000	0x0000	0x0000

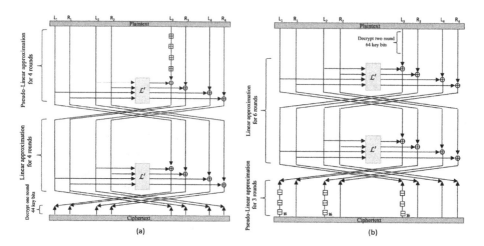

Fig. 4. The Partly-Pseudo-Linear Cryptanalysis on (a) SPARX 128/128 and (b) SPARX 128/256

Table 7. The Partly-Pseudo-Linear Attack on SPARX family

N/K	No. rounds key recovery	Guessed bits	Bias	Data complexity	Time complexity
64/128	9	93	$2^{-15.84}$	2^{32}	2^{125}
128/128	9	98	$2^{-13.73}$	2^{28}	2^{126}
128/256	11	195	$2^{-20.42}$	2^{42}	2^{237}

* N is the block size and K is the key size.

6   Conclusion

We present a new key recovery attack on the SPARX block cipher: Partly-Pseudo-Linear cryptanalysis. We illustrate it by combining linear approximations using the Cho-Pieprzyk property and McKay's pseudo-linear approximations to design a key recovery attack. We are able to recover 93 encryption key bits for 9 rounds of SPARX 64/128, 98 key bits for 9 rounds of SPARX 128/128 and 195 key bits for 11 rounds of SPARX 128/256. We see that we are able to improve on the current literature on linear cryptanalysis of larger variants of SPARX.

We compare our results with those using only Cho-Pieprzyk approximations, extended to key recovery attacks, and observe improvements. For all variants of the SPARX family, we recover more encryption key bits with better bias and lower data complexity by replacing some rounds of Cho-Pieprzyk approximations with pseudo-linear approximations.

Appendix

Table 8 shows the pseudo-linear approximation for the left word of the Sparx 64/128 and same way, we can write the pseudo-linear approximation of the right word. Table 9 shows how the linear mask changes through the 8 rounds. Additionally, for SPARX 128/128 and SPARX 128/256, we can write the pseudo-linear approximation that leads to the active bits of the mask of the linear trail.

Table 8. The pseudo-linear approximation for Partly-pseudo-Linear 9-round attack - Left word of the Sparx 64/128.

Round	Decryption
7	$xl_1^7 = ((xl_3^8 \boxminus ((xr_3^8 \oplus xl_5^8) \ggg 2)) \lll 7) \oplus kl_1^7(12, 14)$
	$xl_2^7 = ((xl_1^8 \boxminus ((xr_1^8 \oplus xl_2^8) \ggg 2)) \lll 7) \oplus kl_2^7(4, 6)$
	$xr_1^7 = ((xl_4^8 \oplus xr_2^8) \ggg 2) \oplus kr_1^7(4, 6)$
8	$xl_1^8 = ((xl_7^9 \boxminus ((xr_5^9 \oplus xl_8^9) \ggg 2)) \lll 7) \oplus kl_1^8(11, 13)$
	$xl_2^8 = ((xl_8^9 \boxminus ((xr_1^9 \oplus xl_1^9) \ggg 2)) \lll 7) \oplus kl_2^8(9, 11)$
	$xl_3^8 = ((xl_2^9 \boxminus ((xr_2^9 \oplus xl_4^9) \ggg 2)) \lll 7) \oplus kl_3^8(3, 5)$
	$xl_4^8 = ((xl_3^9 \boxminus ((xr_3^9 \oplus xl_5^9) \ggg 2)) \lll 7) \oplus kl_4^8(2, 4)$
	$xl_5^8 = ((xl_4^9 \boxminus ((xr_4^9 \oplus xl_6^9) \ggg 2)) \lll 7) \oplus kl_5^8(1, 3)$
	$xr_1^8 = ((xl_5^9 \oplus xr_3^9) \ggg 2) \oplus kr_1^8(9, 11)$
	$xr_2^8 = ((xl_8^9 \oplus xr_5^9) \ggg 2) \oplus kr_2^8(2, 4)$
	$xr_3^8 = ((xl_9^9 \oplus xr_6^9) \ggg 2) \oplus kr_3^8(1, 3)$
9	$NewCR = (CL \oplus CR) \ggg 2$
	$NewCL = (CL \boxminus NewCR) \lll 7$
	$xl_1^9 = NewCL(14, 16) \oplus kl_1^9(14, 16)$
	$xl_2^9 = NewCL(10, 12) \oplus kl_2^9(10, 12)$
	$xl_3^9 = NewCL(9, 11) \oplus kl_3^9(9, 11)$
	$xl_4^9 = NewCL(8, 10) \oplus kl_4^9(8, 10)$
	$xl_5^9 = NewCL(7, 9) \oplus kl_5^9(7, 9)$
	$xl_6^9 = NewCL(6, 8) \oplus kl_6^9(6, 8)$
	$xl_7^9 = NewCL(2, 4) \oplus kl_7^9(2, 4)$
	$xl_8^9 = NewCL(0, 2) \oplus kl_8^9(0, 2)$
	$xl_9^9 = NewCL(15, 17 \bmod 16) \oplus kl_9^9(15, 17 \bmod 16)$
	$xr_1^9 = NewCR(14, 16) \oplus kr_1^9(14, 16)$
	$xr_2^9 = NewCR(8, 10) \oplus kr_2^9(8, 10)$
	$xr_3^9 = NewCR(7, 9) \oplus kr_3^9(7, 9)$
	$xr_4^9 = NewCR(6, 8) \oplus kr_4^9(6, 8)$
	$xr_5^9 = NewCR(0, 2) \oplus kr_5^9(0, 2)$
	$xr_6^9 = NewCR(15, 17 \bmod 16) \oplus kr_6^9(15, 17 \bmod 16)$

Table 9. Linear trail of SPARX 64/128 for 6 rounds – linear key recovery attack.

Round	Cost	Left word				Right word			
		$\lambda_{x^i}^L$	$\lambda_{y^i}^L$	$\lambda_{x^{i+1}}^L$	$\lambda_{y^{i+1}}^L$	$\lambda_{x^i}^R$	$\lambda_{y^i}^R$	$\lambda_{x^{i+1}}^R$	$\lambda_{y^{i+1}}^R$
1	4	0x0000	0x0000	0x0000	0x0000	0x07f8	0xfdf4	0xc7e3	0x37ec
2	5	0x0000	0x0000	0x0000	0x0000	0xc7e3	0x37ec	0x0600	0xc18f
3	1	0x0000	0x0000	0x0000	0x0000	0x0600	0xc18f	0x0603	0x060f
Linear permutation									
4	2	0x0603	0x060f	0x0600	0x000c	0x0000	0x0000	0x0000	0x0000
5	1	0x0600	0x000c	0x000c	0x0000	0x0000	0x0000	0x0000	0x0000
6	1	0x000c	0x0000	0x7800	0x6000	0x0000	0x0000	0x0000	0x0000
Linear permutation									
7	5	0x7818	0x6018	0x7351	0x43a1	0x7800	0x6000	0x8331	0x83c1
8	3	Stop				0x8331	0x83c1	0xe019	0x831f

References

1. Ashur, T., Bodden, D.: Linear Cryptanalysis of Reduced-Round Speck (2016)
2. Bodden, D.: Linear cryptanalysis of reduced-round speck with a heuristic approach: automatic search for linear trails. In: Chen, L., Manulis, M., Schneider, S. (eds.) ISC 2018. LNCS, vol. 11060, pp. 132–150. Springer, Cham (2018). https://doi.org/10.1007/978-3-319-99136-8_8
3. Cho, J.Y., Pieprzyk, J.: Algebraic attacks on SOBER-t32 and SOBER-t16 without stuttering. In: Roy, B., Meier, W. (eds.) FSE 2004. LNCS, vol. 3017, pp. 49–64. Springer, Heidelberg (2004). https://doi.org/10.1007/978-3-540-25937-4_4
4. Cho, J.Y., Pieprzyk, J.: Multiple modular additions and crossword puzzle attack on NLSv2. In: Garay, J.A., Lenstra, A.K., Mambo, M., Peralta, R. (eds.) ISC 2007. LNCS, vol. 4779, pp. 230–248. Springer, Heidelberg (2007). https://doi.org/10.1007/978-3-540-75496-1_16
5. Dinu, D., Perrin, L., Udovenko, A., Velichkov, V., Großschädl, J., Biryukov, A.: Design strategies for ARX with provable bounds: SPARX and LAX. In: Cheon, J.H., Takagi, T. (eds.) ASIACRYPT 2016. LNCS, vol. 10031, pp. 484–513. Springer, Heidelberg (2016). https://doi.org/10.1007/978-3-662-53887-6_18
6. Heys, H.M.: A tutorial on linear and differential cryptanalysis. Cryptologia **26**, 189–221 (2002). https://doi.org/10.1080/0161-110291890885
7. Huang, M., Wang, L.: Automatic search for the linear (hull) characteristics of ARX ciphers: applied to SPECK, SPARX, Chaskey, and CHAM-64. Secur. Commun. Netw. (2020). https://doi.org/10.1155/2020/4898612
8. Liu, Y., Wang, Q., Rijmen, V.: Automatic search of linear trails in ARX with applications to SPECK and Chaskey. In: Manulis, M., Sadeghi, A.-R., Schneider, S. (eds.) ACNS 2016. LNCS, vol. 9696, pp. 485–499. Springer, Cham (2016). https://doi.org/10.1007/978-3-319-39555-5_26
9. Matsui, M.: Linear cryptanalysis method for DES cipher. In: Helleseth, T. (ed.) EUROCRYPT 1993. LNCS, vol. 765, pp. 386–397. Springer, Heidelberg (1994). https://doi.org/10.1007/3-540-48285-7_33

10. McKay, K.A.: Analysis of ARX round functions in secure hash functions. Doctoral Dissertation, The George Washington University, Gelman Library (2014)
11. McKay, K.A., Vora, P.L.: Analysis of ARX functions: pseudo-linear methods for approximation, differentials, and evaluating diffusion. lAGR Gryptology ePrint Archive (2014)
12. Wallén, J.: Linear approximations of addition modulo 2^n. In: Johansson, T. (ed.) FSE 2003. LNCS, vol. 2887, pp. 261–273. Springer, Heidelberg (2003). https://doi.org/10.1007/978-3-540-39887-5_20

Author Index

Printed in the United States
by Bookmasters

Printed in the United States
By Bookmasters